Patty's Journey

The University of Minnesota Press gratefully acknowledges assistance provided for the publication of this volume by the John K. and Elsie Lampert Fesler Fund.

from Orphanage

to Adoption

and Reunion

Patty's Journey

Donna Scott Norling

Afterword by Priscilla Ferguson Clement

University of Minnesota Press   Minneapolis & London

Published by the University of Minnesota Press
111 Third Avenue South, Suite 290
Minneapolis, MN 55401-2520

Printed in the United States of America on acid-free paper

Library of Congress Cataloging-in-Publication Data

Norling, Donna Scott.
    Patty's journey : from orphanage to adoption and reunion / Donna
Scott Norling ; afterword by Priscilla Ferguson Clement.
        p.   cm.
    ISBN 0-8166-2866-1 (hc : acid-free paper)
    I. Title.
PS3564.O5624P38   1996
813'.54—dc20   96-7497

For Glenn
With Love

Faithfulness to the truth of history involves far more than a research, however faithful and scrupulous, into special facts. Such facts may be detailed with the most minute exactness, and yet the narrative, taken as a whole, may be unmeaning or untrue. The narrator must seek to imbue himself with the life and spirit of the time. He must study events in their bearings near and remote; in the character, habits, and manners of those who took part in them. He must himself be, as it were, a sharer or a spectator of the action he describes.

FRANCIS PARKMAN, 1865

Contents

Preface

In the early 1800s, needy children in the United States were incarcerated in almshouses alongside adult paupers, including those who were drunk, venereal, or even insane. Gradually, hundreds of asylums (as the institutions were called) were established to provide temporary care for children (who were labeled inmates).

Later in the century, "orphan trains" began to transport impoverished East Coast children westward to find homes and provide labor for expanding frontiers. By the 1920s, more than two hundred thousand of these children had been "placed out," sometimes lined up on railroad loading docks so prospective parents could pick and choose.

In 1885 Minnesota governor Lucius F. Hubbard, seeking a defining achievement to mark his administration, settled on the child welfare issue. He convinced the state legislature to provide $20,000 to establish, and begin to operate, a state public school. The institution was meant to provide education and temporary shelter for dependent or neglected children until the younger ones could be adopted and the older ones placed in farm homes using indenture contracts, a plan tested during the previous decade in Michigan.

Several Minnesota towns actively sought the state school project for their community. A Steele County site was finally selected because of its location in the midst of the oldest, most populated part of the state. At the junction of two key railroads, it also offered 160 acres for buildings and farming. With the children's labor, the crops and animals could provide food for the school and some extra profit to help with other expenses.

By the time the first three "cottages," to house thirty-five children each, had been erected, the funding was exhausted. It looked as though the buildings would stand vacant until the next appropriation, but the citizens of Owatonna offered an advance of $5,000. The school admitted the first three children on December 2, 1886, and eighteen more arrived before Christmas Eve. The formal dedication of the buildings took place several months later.

On a sunny, festive day, all the state's dignitaries gathered in the small southern-Minnesota town to celebrate the official opening of the new State Public School for Dependent and Neglected Children. The *Owatonna Journal and Herald*'s headline for August 12, 1887, declared that "Heaven Smiled and the People Rejoiced." The lead article told of bands and flags, bountiful food, and twenty-five hundred celebrating people. The newspaper described the new institution's mission in the language of the time:

> The school is but the nursery, as it were, to prepare these little waifs for transplanting into wholesome Christian homes. Its office is to gather in and preserve those neglected little ones who would otherwise perish on the dusty roadsides or be choked by the rank weeds in an uncultivated soil.

The real stories began after the cheering throngs deserted the littered grounds and children continued to fill the large, fortresslike buildings. Some of the "state public schoolers" remained there until they were eighteen and found military or civilian employment. Many were indentured to farms or households while they were still young teenagers. (Minnesota's initial indenture contract specified that the child would receive kind treatment, at least four months of schooling each year, and training for a useful occupation. When the contract expired, usually at age eighteen, the child was to be paid seventy-five to one hundred dollars and given two suits of clothing. Even those modest conditions were not always met.) Other children were adopted, sometimes in midchildhood, with widely varying results.

This deeply personal account of one of those journeys begins fifty years after the school's opening day. It attempts to preserve some history of that quasi orphanage before it is lost to time and fading memories.

Although one story can't capture all the children's experiences, it explores some elements common to displaced children—the power of their pasts, the clarity and longevity of their early memories, the shadow child that often haunts them. And it illustrates that even adoption, often viewed as a panacea, is really a fragile, lifelong process.

A Taste of Home

Excitement was rare and precious in 1936. Grown-ups talked often about the Great Depression, which I sometimes pictured as fog: silent, invasive. Other times, it was a tornado in painfully slow motion, shattering dreams, uprooting families, sucking the smiles from their faces and scattering them somewhere above the clouds.

But on a sticky-hot morning I remember clearly, our small Minneapolis apartment overflowed with the gleeful energy of two small girls. My sister had just turned six; I was "going on four."

Yvonne and I were having a tug-of-war over a new box of cereal. The struggle started at the table, and soon both box and children landed on the linoleum floor. In the tangle of arms and legs, the wide sailor collar on my dress flipped into a hood. My heel, digging in like an anchor, untied my shoelace. When I captured the box for a moment, I stared in wonder at the Dionne quintuplets, the country's darlings, posing wide-eyed on the front panel.

"Enough now, Yvonne, Patty—or I'll take the box from both of you.'' We handed it over long enough for Momma to read the offer on the back. Child-size spoons! Each handle bore the name of a quintuplet—and her likeness, since the Canadian two-year-olds were not identical. I was jealous that Yvonne had a ''quint'' with her own name. I would have to choose among the others: Marie, Cécile, Émilie, and Annette. I finally chose Cécile, although Yvonne suggested Annette for my middle name, Ann. Probably because I hadn't thought of it first, I stuck to Cécile.

Each spoon cost ten cents and a cereal box top. Momma hesitated to commit that much money plus a three-cent stamp just for extra spoons, but she was weary from her third pregnancy, and her daughters were determined. She cautioned us not to tell Daddy about her extravagant promise when he returned from his daily job search. Then she filled out the coupon, put it in an envelope with the box top, and placed it in a drawer to await the coins and another box top. She probably vowed to buy only cereals with free premiums inside for the duration of the Depression.

I first knew we didn't have enough money when Momma said we couldn't buy raisins. She knew I loved them; she would add handfuls to my cereal flakes. She also baked them into the rice pudding she pulled steaming from the oven. Then she sprinkled cinnamon over the top before she set it on the table to cool a little while we ate our soup.

We still had plenty of books. Momma got them from the library a few blocks away. She'd sit between us on our green frieze couch and read about exciting journeys, huge oceans, and comical creatures— puffins and koalas—while two pairs of bright blue eyes devoured every illustration. She promised to take us to the zoo some day soon, but we would have to ride three streetcars to get to Como Park in St. Paul.

The summer of 1936 was beastly hot in the Twin Cities. During the worst three weeks, in July, the temperature soared to between 90 and 108 degrees every day. Waves of heat shimmered in the air.

Even we children, usually able to slumber away in a pool of sweat, sought relief outside our sweltering apartment. We searched for a night breeze on the front steps, or on the flat rooftop of our building. Damp bangs clung to my high forehead like corn silk clinging to the husk. Momma promised I could have barrettes as soon as the wispy strands that brushed my face were thick enough to hold them. Then I would grow my hair long, like Momma's, down past my shoulders.

Lately, it seemed Momma was sick most of the time. Her eyes, so transparent, always the barometer of her unspoken feelings, were often cloudy or misty now. She was a tiny, pale woman who sometimes appeared more fragile than her daughters, relying on Daddy's strength as much as we did.

Some days, our family found an hour of respite from the heat in the bar beneath our apartment, where portable fans hummed as they circulated the damp smoky air. Our parents drank beer, and we sipped cold Orange Crush from sweating contoured bottles. Yvonne and I scrunched small in the corners of the booth, occasionally bothering each other with an extended foot until we were ordered to stop.

Tempers ran hot, too, during this torrid spell. Normally, small children our age, black and white, played marbles and hopscotch or jumped rope together impartially in the street. Older kids, picking up cues from adults, had learned to divide along color lines when disputes arose.

One day, Yvonne and I watched from the sidelines while a row of white kids in front of us taunted a group of black youths gathered across the street. Storefront signs behind them framed their dark faces, turned hard with fear and anger.

The young voices nearer us boiled with hate.

''Nigger!''

''Jungle bunnies!''

''Stupid savages!''

I saw the broken wedge of brick leave a black hand; I spun away and saw Yvonne slump to the step, blood covering the side of her head. I pulled her to her feet and hurried her up our flight of stairs, both of us screaming. Momma put Yvonne's head under the kitchen faucet. The water ran red; I thought my sister would lose all her blood and crumple to the floor like an empty pillowcase. Finally, Momma raised Yvonne's head, pressed a clean dish towel against the cut, and wrapped a bath towel around it.

"Stop crying, Patty Ann. Go downstairs and find someone who can take us to the hospital." My heart was pounding. I was shaking and felt so weak, I took the steep stairs sitting down.

⌒ ⌒

In time, Yvonne's blond curls, her greatest source of pride, grew back over the wound where the brick grazed her head, but we were more cautious now, playing in our neighborhood. Our parents no longer let us go alone to the park a few blocks away, to travel its curving paths on metal roller skates clamped to sturdy shoes while the keys to tighten them swung against our ribs from strings around our necks.

By the time Momma mailed the completed spoon envelope, thanks to some temporary employment Daddy found with the WPA, summer was over. We waited impatiently for our magical silver spoons, unaware that Momma had put them away for Christmas when it became clear that there would be no money for toys. There would be no pretense of Santa Claus that year, then, because we knew our only gift came from the cereal company, not the North Pole.

At the time, all I knew about President Franklin Roosevelt's new program, the Works Progress Administration, was that its jobs were too scarce despite all the hospitals, libraries, parkways, and golf courses the WPA workers would build. Daddy's skills were mechanical, but I heard him agree with the president's decision to fund the WPA's Federal Art Project.

"Why not?" Roosevelt said. "Artists and musicians are human beings. They have to live." My painter grandfather worked for a time in the mural division, commissioned to paint scenes on a post office wall.

On Christmas Eve, we had popcorn and cider, and a wonderful meal! Momma made something called "birds without wings," rice and hamburger rolled up in cabbage leaves and covered with stewed tomatoes. We had squash too. Like the cabbage and tomatoes, it was from the final harvest of Grandpa's garden, stored in his cool basement for this special occasion. He had been out of permanent work longer than Daddy, but the garden that he and Grandma tended behind their stucco house yielded vegetables and berries alongside two apple trees.

Christmas carols flowed from the radio in the living room, and from the oven came the scent of dessert, baked apples, their cores replaced with brown sugar, butter—and raisins! Momma basted them with the caramely sauce.

''The center is very hot,'' she said as she poured chilled cream over them at the table.

I knew Momma wished Aunt Ruth had invited us to her home, where there would be a tree, and cookies and cocoa for the children. But she reminded herself aloud that it would be a bother for them to drive us. And anyway, her sister's family would want to enjoy their gifts and holiday dinner alone. I was sure Momma wouldn't have felt that way, because she always told us how important it was to share, to consider each other's feelings. Neither of Aunt Ruth's children liked to share.

We were delighted with our spoons and used them not as utensils but as dolls, walking and talking, while small fingers held them carefully by the narrow curve above the shiny bowl. Except for the bas-relief images of Cécile and Yvonne Dionne near the tips of the handles, the spoons were smooth, and much brighter than our tableware. We laughed to see our faces, distorted and upside down, in their silver bowls.

Yvonne's cereal box photo was tacked above the table that held our old wooden radio. I had cut mine into five paper dolls, none with a complete anatomy because of their overlapping positions in the picture. I made clothes for them from any scrap of paper or cloth I could find. Our color crayons were worn away long ago, but I learned by accident that some foods—canned blueberries and beets were good—could be used to make colored hearts or flowers on the doll clothes. Momma was upset to find a corner missing from the worn oilcloth that covered our kitchen table. That triangle made a pointed hat for one quint, decorated with a jaunty feather I worked out of my pillow.

Two days after Christmas, Aunt Ruth and her children, Johnny and Jeanie, did arrive with a birthday present for me: a white fur muff shaped like a kitten's head. (It became a ball for Yvonne and me to toss back and forth. I knew better than to wear it outside our door.)

While Momma and her sister chatted, Daddy took all four children to *Snow White and the Seven Dwarfs* for my special birthday surprise! It was wonderful just walking the blocks to the theater, following Daddy's easy stride. I tried to walk in the footprints he left in the light dusting of new snow. Soon, tired of leaning into his widely spaced tracks, I ran ahead to take his hand.

"A pinch to grow an inch," he said, and pinched my finger as he slowed his pace. "Maybe we should give you a few extra pinches?" he said, referring to my short stature.

The theater was packed for this new animated film. I was terrified of the stepmother witch but enchanted by the story. Afterward, Daddy bought a bag of hamburgers at the Band Box, ten for a quarter. At home, we heated them up again and ate them, one for each child and two for grown-ups, with big glasses of milk. Grandma had sent cookies over with Aunt Ruth, and four candles to poke into mine. I didn't want this birthday to end. When it did, I slept peacefully. No witches, just pretty music and dancing in my head:

> Some DAY my prince will come,
> Lah LAH, la la la la—

Winter dragged on. Yvonne and I huddled in our bed at night to stay warm. By day, our bed became the couch that Daddy occupied often now. His tall slender frame was restless even in repose, but he always drew us like a magnet. He still played our games, pretending sleep, then a quick grab around our waist and a firm hold while we squealed and tried to wiggle loose. But sometimes his eyes were wet, and his whiskers felt sharp even in the middle of the day.

"God damn it, Judy," he said suddenly one day, "I can't take this shit any more!"

"Don't you think these children hear enough swearing on the street, Al?" she said, before he slammed out the door.

I wanted my playful parents back, not these two who argued more and more. Where was the man who used to toss aside the throw rugs to dance with his wife around the floor of our living room? And the woman who moved gracefully on tiptoe, her face against his chest, while Yvonne and I mocked them by dancing and giggling in the corner?

It had been months since they talked about the house we would buy, with a yard, and a big tree where Daddy would hang a tire swing the minute we moved in. They rarely even talked about the baby now, but we knew it was coming soon because people would ask us "Do you have your new baby yet?" and Momma had a hard time bending over.

One evening, Daddy talked quietly with two men in our living room, men with serious unfamiliar faces, men he must have met on a recent job. Momma tended to Yvonne and me while we splashed in our footed bathtub. Afterward, I ran to Daddy in my flannel nightgown, interrupting his conversation. He boosted me up high by the ceiling, pivoting me back and forth.

"Where's my good night kiss?" He lowered me slowly so I could plant it on his cheek. "Did you have fun today, Patsy?" he asked, baiting me with the nickname that made me wrinkle my nose. Chubby arms circling his neck, I buried my face in his shoulder, certain I could still smell the sun.

It had warmed Daddy and me this first glorious spring day as we walked to the grocery store, after he finally arose late in the morning. I'd been waiting impatiently for this promised outing, just for him and me.

We chose meats from the glass case—sliced ham and, for me, bologna.

"Ba-lon-ee?" Daddy said. "But you're already full of baloney!"

We scooped pickles from a barrel, and the aproned man sliced a fat loaf of bread. Daddy finished buying cold pop (sold then only in bottles, with refundable deposits) and mustard, while I stared at a pie in the showcase—creamy pale yellow with fluffy whipped topping, sprinkled with coconut.

"We'll take the cherry pie," Daddy told the grocer. "We're going on a picnic." Well, I thought, you can't have everything.

In the sun again, we walked up the stairs to street level. I carried the pie carefully by sturdy string crisscrossed around the tan box. (It hadn't yet occurred to anyone that the aesthetics of a bleached white box was worth extra expense and pollution.)

At home I helped make sandwiches, and we packed everything into our big wicker laundry basket, the cold bottles of cola and orange around the edges, newspaper and a blanket over the top. Momma packed our thick white plates into a shopping bag, with cloth napkins in between, but her mood didn't match ours. Yvonne was trying to sample everything, and now Momma slapped the fingers that tugged at the pie box.

"No dessert before your food," she said angrily.

But that night, when Daddy smoothed my nightgown as he rolled me off his shoulder into a chair, I remembered the sweet cherry taste in my mouth, the tickle of grass on my bare feet, leaping high to catch the ball Daddy lobbed to Yvonne and me over and over. I recalled Momma, finally relaxed, napping in the speckled shade of a budded tree, her borrowed dress with snaps let out now at the waist, gathered up to bare her white legs to the sun.

My memories were interrupted by a knock and shout at our door. Two uniformed policemen burst in and put double bracelets on Daddy and the other two men. I heard snatches of talk, something about radios, and then they were gone, and Momma slumped into a chair and sobbed out loud into her apron.

⌒ ⌒

A huge statue of a reclining man, old and nearly naked, dominated the vast rotunda of the stone courthouse that contained the county jail. His big toe was larger than my hand; his bare leg rested on a ferocious alligator. I stared at the bearded man while Momma pulled us to the elevators. Above their doors, a row of gargoyles leered down at me, shockingly grotesque to my artless eyes.

Inside the crowded cage, Momma's hand guarded my shoulder from a cigarette dangling carelessly from a hairy hand. The elevator jerked to a stop a few times before we reached our floor and stepped into cooler air.

Momma had promised Yvonne and me a visit with Daddy, but we could barely see him behind the heavy screen. A "visit" with Daddy without touching him, hugging him, was like putting food just beyond the reach of a starving person. I hated it so much that I met his uneasy questions with a stony silence.

When I finally arrived home after a carsick ride on the streetcar, I tore up my five quints and threw Cécile across the room.

"Goddam, sonna-bitch, geejus cripes." I tried to recall every bad word I'd heard in the streets. Yvonne, afraid to even try to comfort me, curled up in a chair and whimpered quietly. Momma moved slowly around the kitchen, preparing a supper none of us would eat.

Later, Momma broke the stillness and gathered us against her. We waited for a long moment while she mustered her energy and courage. "The judge has decided that Daddy will have to go away for a while," she said softly.

"Go where?" we asked in unison.

"To a different jail," she said, pulling her hand from around my waist to reach into her pocket for a handkerchief.

I felt weak. Yvonne asked the next question before I could think of it.

"But why?" she asked in a pleading voice, her face pushed into a tight scowl. "What did he do?"

"He . . . listened to the wrong friends," she said haltingly, "and he helped them break into a store. They took radios." She shrugged and was silent.

Yvonne persisted. "What for? We *have* a radio."

Momma's small laugh sounded hollow in the charged room. She hugged her older daughter. "I know, love." She paused, then continued very slowly. "They wanted to sell the radios to get money— money for the baby—for—." Her voice cracked and rose; she stood and walked toward the dark window. With her shoulders slumped, she looked so tiny, even to me. I ran to grasp her around her legs. She turned and I buried my face against her stomach, full and ripe as a watermelon. The fear that welled up inside me came from a deeper place than any I'd known before.

The final question hung in the air, because neither Yvonne nor I dared to ask Momma: For how long?

A few miserable days later, I woke up early in the morning to find our neighbor from across the hall, the one with the pretty name, drinking coffee at our kitchen table. Winona Starbird told me Momma had gone to the hospital to have our new baby. We waited all day, and finally—"You have a little brother," Mrs. Starbird said when she returned from the telephone in the bar downstairs. "And Judith is fine. She and Duane will be home in a week or so." (A brief maternity stay, in those years.)

Children were not allowed to visit the hospital. With Daddy away, it was hard to be separated from Momma. Our week at Aunt Ruth's house dragged. Her lawn was just turning green, and she "preferred" that we not play on it. Her kids preferred that we not use their trikes and wagons on the sidewalk, either, so we swung on the chain-suspended bench on the porch until its wooden slats left stripes on the backs of our short legs, and we wondered excitedly about our new brother.

Aunt Ruth's house was immaculate. The meals she served to the four of us children, and Uncle Willard when he was home, were similar enough to Momma's cooking to be comforting. But Yvonne and I were surprised how often she corrected our manners. We didn't know we shouldn't pick up our forks until she lifted hers, or that we had to ask to be excused before leaving the table.

At night, in the double bed in Aunt Ruth's guest room, we'd wonder why she refused our offers to set the table, why she asked us to stay out of her children's bedrooms. We whispered about our aunt and uncle's twin beds and their polite, reserved manner with each other.

Finally, we were home, with a real live doll to help bathe and dress! Duane was bald and chubby with deep creases at his elbows, wrists, and knees. When we cooed at him, he kicked hard and blew through his closed lips so they flubbered, "b-h-r-r-r." Although Yvonne and I rarely fought (because she backed down so easily), we argued now for the right to comfort him when he cried. We showed him off proudly to visitors and took turns unwrapping the rattles, bibs, and undershirts they brought. As soon as Daddy comes home, I thought, everything will be perfect.

But Momma still cried all the time. I thought it was about Daddy, or that she was tired from nighttime feedings, until one day she said, "Yvonne, Patty Ann, we have to go to court today, and you have to be very good and very brave.'' Her words barely prepared us for another trip past the foreboding Father of Waters statue, let alone the trauma of being separated from our mother.

This time the elevator in the big stone courthouse brought us not to Daddy but to a large room with benches, a gray-haired man in a black robe, and other men in suits.

Yvonne and I sat, still and expectant in our best dresses, the scuffs on our oxford shoes covered with brown polish. I wanted to hear more about Daddy's sentence, find out when he was coming home. Instead they seemed to be talking about Yvonne, Duane, and me, and who should take care of us. I didn't know what the word *dependency* meant, but it was clearly the reason they took us out the door, while Momma reached out for us and an awful silent cry turned her face into a mask that I would never forget.

In time, I would be haunted by another memory. The woman who spoke from the front of the courtroom, the one with the plume in her hat, was the same woman who had come to our apartment on two occasions. Once she spoke to Momma, then asked Yvonne and me a few questions. Momma was upset after she left and told us not to tell her anything if she came again. On her second visit, she found seven-year-old Yvonne taking care of Duane and me. Momma had told us exactly where she was going for a short time, but when the woman asked if we knew where she was, we clamped our lips and shook our heads. I would have years to wonder if, trying to follow our mother's instructions, we had lied our way into the clutches of the authorities.

Now the court had moved, with a speed that left Momma unprepared, to take her three children from her. If Momma had had warnings, she must have denied the reality of them, or surely she would have told us that her inability to provide for us could result in our becoming wards of the state.

Under Minnesota law, no proof of abuse or neglect was necessary to ''rescue'' us from our home, with its meager material resources (their term was *indigent*). I would be left with small memories—spoons and cabbages, cherries and stone—all awash now in the taste of my salty tears.

Owatonna State Public School

No one ever keeps a secret
so well as a child.
VICTOR HUGO

On the night of my fifth birthday I discovered I could fly. I'd tried
before, but this time it just happened.

It was December 27, 1937. My home now was the fifty-year-old
State Public School for Dependent and Neglected Children in a small
Minnesota town called Owatonna. Legend states that frail, sickly
Owatonna, daughter of the great chief Wabena, was restored to
health by the *minnewaucan* (curative waters) at the edge of town.

That December evening, while supper dishes were cleared from
our long table, a woman from a local service club gave me a tooth-
brush wrapped in white tissue paper and a big red apple. Those gifts
and five candles on my cupcake acknowledged the date I'd been delivered to parents who were now absent from my life.

"Let's sing 'Happy Birthday' to Patricia," our volunteer visitor said brightly to the other children. They responded merrily through mouths ringed with pink frosting. While the other children applauded their own singing, I noticed the man slouched against the door frame. His was the only somber face in the room. He wore a matching gray shirt and pants, and his limp brown hair lay in oily strands across one brow. He raked it back with his fingers, exposing a pimply forehead. Maybe he noticed me, of all the little innocents around the table, simply because of the attention being paid to me. Or maybe I stared at the custodian, wishing he would go back to his chores.

Late that night, I hovered near the ceiling and watched his hands on the small form below. Patty lay silent and motionless on her narrow cot, his hand over her mouth. Nor did any sound come from the child (asleep?) on the other cot a few feet away, separated only by a tall metal locker standing guard between the beds. Nor from the partially open doorway to a dimly lit hall on the other side of Patty's cot. The darkness held only his whispered threats, the rustle of hands moving roughly under the covers.

Suspended in time and space, I hung there for whatever minutes he decided it would be, my only defense this magical airborne retreat. As soon as the janitor, still breathing heavily, disappeared into the hallway, I floated back to Patty's limp form, damp and cold inside the scratchy white nightgown. I tucked the blanket around us, tried to stop her trembling. Finally her quiet sobs gave way to exhausted sleep despite the pain.

☞ ☜

No doubt I had become skilled at detachment. I had practiced that form of control ever since my arrival more than two months ago.

On that October morning, I slid from the sedan's back seat, stepped onto its running board, and jumped to the ground. Not as carsick as usual, after riding most of the seventy-five miles from Minneapolis with my head in my sister's lap, I was still grateful for crisp fresh air. The light brown hair I'd planned to grow long was cut square now into bangs and a Buster Brown bob. I shivered in my thin summer coat, and Yvonne grasped my hand and led me toward the white admissions building.

It looked like a large house, two stories high, with a porch on each side. The woman who walked beside us, carrying our baby brother Duane, wore a black hat atop her bun of hair, and a black coat. She was the tallest woman I had ever seen.

While our driver moved his car away from the walk, two women in blue uniform dresses met us at the door. One led Yvonne away, saying only, "You'll see each other later." Yvonne twisted to see me. Her eyes, wide and scared now, looked as dark blue as mine, but her face was narrower, more vulnerable, framed with her wispy curls.

"Where is my sister going?" I asked the tall woman, who ignored me as she hurried down the hall with Duane, awake now and crying. She held him across her arms like a ticking time bomb.

I tried to follow, but the other blue dress stopped me and led me to a small kitchen. Eating lunch alone, I finished my Jell-O and milk but pushed aside the sandwich, filled with something gray I didn't recognize.

I was turned over to a white dress who helped me out of my clothes and plopped me abruptly into a running shower that took my breath away. Suds and water stung my eyes as white dress shook shampoo on my head. At home, in our claw-footed bathtub, I'd played with small jars and a metal strainer until my fingers were white and wrinkled and the water began to feel cold. Then Momma would lift me out and pat me dry.

"Patty Ann Prune," she would tease, and kiss a puckered fingertip. But now this stranger rubbed me briskly and slipped a gown up my arms. Other women took over, checked me for everything from head lice to foot fungus, stuck me with needles, then had me hop, skip, and jump. Next they watched me do puzzles—silly baby games—dropping square pegs into square holes. They told me I was very smart. I believed it, not because I trusted them, but because Daddy had told me I was.

"Better to be short physically than mentally," he'd concede. Still, he would coax me to eat "so you stretch those little legs out."

A man in a white coat flicked a small rubber hammer against my knee. His examination was proceeding slowly from my ears to my ankles. When he finished, he boosted me down from the table and abruptly shed his quiet, intense manner. Smiling broadly, he began asking many questions. Some, I was sure, were already answered in the stack of papers by his elbow.

"How old are you, Patricia?"

"Do you have any brothers and sisters?"

"Do you have any 'owies'—any place that hurts?" I answered no.

"Do you have any questions about why you're here?" Not knowing where to begin, I shook my head.

After standing still for some X-ray photographs, I was sent to play on one of the screened porches with other newly arrived girls and boys. My "luggage"—a flour sack with a drawstring through the top, devised for my stay at Aunt Ruth's house—was returned to me. Momma had hemmed it and showed me how a closed safety pin on the end of a string would help me guide the string through the hem. Inside, a few clothes, books, and my worn rag doll, Alice. A boy, bigger than me, tried to grab my things, so I showed him how we protected our property on the tough streets where I'd lived.

"Ah-h! Gee!" he moaned, doubling over. As soon as he could straighten up, he limped off to tattle to the matron. I could tell by her face, and the way she squeezed my arm, that she wasn't interested in my reason.

"Roughneck!" she said, then made me sit on the stairs in a hallway. I puzzled over her word, one I hadn't heard before. I rubbed my smooth neck and wondered at the way adults express themselves.

After what seemed like a week, I heard loud excited voices on the porch and saw a red glow through the doorway. A building, separated from us by a large grassy field, was ablaze. I crept in to watch with the others, fascinated by the fire's yellow and orange fingers poking at a mottled gray sky and the firefighters' frenzied movements silhouetted against the flames.

Soon I was discovered (by the same crabby matron) and sent back to my lonely step. I thought she'd have forgotten about me by now.

The small window in the front door darkened; now the hall's only light came from adjoining rooms. When my hands tired from making shadow animals on the wall, I sprawled across the bottom step. A younger matron nearly tripped over me.

"Why are you sitting alone?" she asked.

"I don't know," I said. (Because that mean old bag told me to, I thought.)

She led me to a seat at a long table where, by now, the other new-comers had begun to eat their chocolate pudding desserts. Suddenly, I felt humiliated for being punished, furious because the bully I'd kneed earlier was sneering at me, and terribly anxious because Yvonne was still nowhere in sight. I stubbornly refused to eat the meal set before me, although I felt starved and the cabbage stew and crusty bread smelled good.

"We always eat what we are served here," said the plump, gray-haired woman who removed my full plate. Then she lowered her voice and said kindly, "But I know it feels strange at first."

It took all my resolve to hold back tears that burned behind my eyes. A different uniform (where did they all come from?) asked polite questions that I didn't answer while she helped me change into a hard white gown. I wanted my soft flannel one, blue, like my sister's pink one, that Momma gave me. I hated them, I wanted to die. Momma, Momma!

New-uniform boosted me into a crib—a crib!—saying I could have a bed when one was available. I'd have slept on a pile of rocks if Yvonne could be with me. I risked having the dam burst wide open by giving voice to just three words:

"Where's my sister?" I asked in a husky voice.

"We'll find her tomorrow," she said cheerfully, then left me to soak my pillow in the dark room. Sometime in the night, I soaked their nightgown and crib too, a new habit that would continue sporadically for a long time.

⌒ ⌒

All new arrivals (and returned runaways, if they'd been gone more than three days) had to be quarantined for three weeks in the admissions and medical building, so it housed both boys and girls, as did the nursery building where our brother Duane lived. In all the other residential units on the state school's campus, children were segregated by gender. But both men and women were employed in all the portentous brick dormitories (incongruously called cottages) that circled the grounds behind a larger brick administration building.

On the December morning after I was molested on my cot by a male employee, I didn't have to search for Yvonne. We were housed in the same building and took meals on the same shift in the administration building's dining hall. She appeared at my breakfast table as soon as she'd finished her own meal with the other seven-year-olds. She knew she was supposed to stay with her group, but she also knew this was cornmeal mush day, and I would be sitting alone at my table.

"You can leave when you've finished all your cereal," the matron had said as usual, and left the room while I stuck out my tongue at her broad back. It wouldn't do any good to tell her again that it made me puke. She would only say, "That's 'regurgitate,' Patty." I was surprised that grown-ups would make up such a hard word when there was already a little word that said it so plainly. Besides, with my heavy lisp and a loose tooth, it was all I could do to say "puke."

Yvonne quickly swallowed down the cold lumpy mess in my bowl. How could she do it? It almost made me sick just to watch her.

"Patty! Your shoulders are shivering." She tried to get the *s* words out, but the family lisp won.

I'd planned to be as tough and profane as the bigger kids in our old neighborhood when I told her about the night before.

"That guy with all the k-keys on his belt is a b-b-big mean s-shit!" I didn't want to cry; somehow it would make him win again, but I nearly drowned my sister when she held my face against her blouse. Even after I lost the emotional support of parents, I'd retained a feeling of physical sturdiness. My child legs seemed always planted firmly against the harsh winds of change. But today, even my skin felt charged by inner turmoil. Yvonne's hand rubbing my back was more touch than I could bear.

"No, don't!" I said and pulled away. Her eyes flashed. "Did he hurt you?" A laugh escaped me in short bursts. That seemed to confuse and alarm my sister even more.

I wanted to make *his* skin crawl, too. Find him and push him into a pond full of snakes. And maybe one of those slimy creatures with a big head and eight wiggly legs that I'd seen in a nature movie.

Yvonne was fascinated with the part about me flying, but when I tried to demonstrate, I couldn't do it. Still, I knew I hadn't dreamt it. I could still remember the feeling—detached, light as a feather, floating free.

Yvonne took me to the office, where we waited to see the head matron. ("Her Majesty" in our private conversations, because she walked so straight in her silk dresses and wore her braided hair like a crown. She was serene and pleasant, but she seemed to swish among us like an observant alien, visiting from a calmer planet.) She listened while Yvonne said, "My sister is five now. She doesn't have to be with the little kids." We "little kids," postnursery but not yet five, were assigned to one of several double bedrooms off the main floor's long hallway.

I'd heard that this arrangement made it easier to isolate small children, with their frequent childhood illnesses, and to accommodate uneven sleep patterns and late night potty habits.

"We have to wait until there is space upstairs," Her Majesty told Yvonne, "and anyway, Patricia won't be in the same dorm as you, because there are so many of you seven-year-olds."

I could see Yvonne was ready to burst. "I know," her head moved up and down, blond curls bouncing, "but when can she come to second floor?"

Despite the anxiety that raged inside us, we conformed to that mysterious but predominant response of abused children—at least those who haven't been taught to tell. Neither of us divulged my terrible secret, even when H.M. said the change wouldn't be made until spring.

⌒ ⌒

At bedtime, all the girls in our building sat on metal folding chairs around the perimeter of the large room we played in by day. Each child was handed a long white nightgown with her name printed on a tape in the neckline.

"P. Pearson!" a matron called out, and I scrambled to the center of the room to claim my bleach-hard gown with its stiff folds that hung in gathers from a shoulder yoke. As we'd been taught, we slipped the full gowns over our heads, then let them hang from our shoulders while we modestly undressed under cover.

We took our places in alphabetical order, so Yvonne undressed next to me. The ritual felt strange to us—accustomed to flinging off our clothes in a race to be first into our soft gowns and under our faded but cherished homemade quilt, two girls who had shared a bathtub, smacking hands against the water while we pedaled against each other's feet. So we would feign modesty, gasping and covering our eyes if we caught a glimpse of thigh, or we'd teasingly flick our hemlines above our knees.

We started to disrobe on a voice signal from the matron after the last child received her gown. Invariably, Yvonne would finish before me, then raise her long gown's neckline to fall on hands clasped on top of her head, and with elbows stuck in the sleeves move the headless gown back and forth. Her "ghost" trick never failed to make me giggle, until the matron said, "Quiet, girls. It's time to say our prayer."

Our prayer was the Twenty-third Psalm, recited dutifully and mechanically every evening. I had scant religious background; Momma had just begun to send Yvonne and me to Sunday school at the nearby Covenant Tabernacle, where a kind woman named Esther Jenson told us incredible stories about men named Noah, Jonah, and Moses. But this Psalm prayer was unfamiliar until the matrons had us memorize it by repeating each line after them. With no explanation of the verses' meaning, I could only put them in the context of my own experience. So I felt uncomfortable now saying "He maketh me to lie down in green pastures." I couldn't begin to pronounce words like *anointest*, and I wondered about this Shirley who would follow me all the days of my life.

☞   ☜

While we waited for my spring move, my sister began to stuff her bed after the first bed check. Then she'd sneak down back stairs carrying Alice, so if she was caught she could say she forgot to give her to me at bedtime. Yvonne slept crowded on my cot, dropping onto the wood floor if she heard someone coming. My roommate didn't have to ask why or be warned not to tell. We were all members of a sisterhood who learned survival tactics at a remarkably tender age.

One morning, a matron shook Yvonne awake and sent her upstairs with a stern warning to stay there. But by then, my sister-protector had taken care of mister key man. He came slinking in one night and had already knelt by my bed when a long white nightgown with no head above it rose, swaying, from the floor on the other side of the bed. After his quick retreat, Yvonne and I cried and laughed into the night, clinging to each other and planning for my move to the second floor.

The news came on Valentine's Day, so we thought this must be "spring." Her Majesty came down to the playroom herself to inform me. "Patricia," she said, her arm around my shoulder, "we have a bed and locker for you on second floor west. Please move your things today, as a new girl will be moving into your room after supper." My heart flipped over once for this unsuspecting "new girl" before relief washed over me from head to toe.

I raced to pack the few possessions in my locker and hug Franny, the shy girl who had shared my room. I promised to lend her Yvonne to agitate for her move upstairs as soon as she reached her fifth birthday in June. A box had been placed on my bed, just big enough for my clothes and toys. Still small for my age, I could barely get my arms around the filled box. With my eyes peeking over the top, I hurried back down the hall. I saw the janitor in my path, saw the look on his face but not the pole he stuck in front of my feet.

I don't remember the fall, or even the pain from my bumped head and twisted knee. But I remember H.M.'s words: "We're going to delay your move because the stairs will be hard until you get rid of that elastic bandage." And I remember hop-skipping stiff legged over to the stairs and sitting on the bottom step while both hands pushed down on the step behind me and my good leg boosted my rump, a step at a time. H.M. must have sensed my desperation because she agreed to let me sleep upstairs, although I would take all daily activities on the main floor, to make trips to the dining hall easier, until I was fully recovered.

My fall was recorded as an accident. The child whose turn it was to scrub the twenty-foot hallway had left a pail in my path, they said. It would be useless to argue; half the school's employees were related. But my "accident" resulted in a visit from Momma and Aunt Ruth. Momma hadn't been able to find a ride from Minneapolis to Owatonna since before Christmas (something about dangerous roads), although she was allowed to see us once a month. Now she brought us each a large doll. Yvonne's was Shirley Temple, and mine was Jane Withers. Yvonne took hers to a distant chair and hid her tears of excitement while she stroked the blond curls. My hands trembled, feeling my doll's shoes and soft dress while her serene eyes looked up at me.

Even these new treasures couldn't compete with our other surprise. Baby Duane, whom Yvonne and I could visit once a month in his building, was brought in to see Momma and—just since our last playtime with him—he was walking! He was shy at first, in new surroundings, but finally gave me a lovely wet kiss. Aunt Ruth talked more than all of us. No one would directly answer my questions about Daddy, so I figured he was still behind that screen. Momma sniffled so much she could barely finish reading the card Grandma sent to us, with two embroidered handkerchiefs enclosed. I didn't know what Momma wanted me to say to make her feel better. I was sure she didn't want to hear about my birthday night.

Years later, I would pinpoint this day as one of crucial change—perhaps in Momma's understanding of her parental rights? Although the facility where I lived was often referred to as an orphanage, most of the children had one or two parents who had been judged incapable of supporting them. Many of these parents did not realize, when their children were committed to the state school, that the court proceedings made each child a ward of the state and canceled all parental rights.

But now, I believed we just had to wait until they let Daddy leave that place. Then he would come for us.

A new girl, Elaine, had asked a woman (a visitor who didn't work here, judging by her sweater and skirt) why she couldn't live with her grandma. I had given up asking that kind of question, and was surprised when Elaine's was answered.

"Relatives," the woman said, "are not allowed to adopt kids." I was sure I'd never understand the rules grown-ups made. Then I realized, with a deep sense of abandonment, that I had no idea whether any of mine had even tried.

Everyone said I was "the spittin' image" of Aunt Ruth, the youngest of Momma's three sisters, and the one who lived closest. I couldn't see myself in her delicate fair features, and the comments about our resemblance didn't seem to overwhelm her, either. She did insist that I had inherited my artistic ability from her, although it was Grandpa who helped me with my drawing. More important, it was Grandpa I tried to please—because I knew he liked me, the way children always know. When our "trouble" started, nearly a year before, most of our relatives were still mixed up in my mind, a tangle of names and who belongs in which family, the way it is unless you care enough to make time together. Our grandparents, I believed, wanted us, but maybe their age and finances prevented it as much as the law did.

I missed Grandpa's lap and Grandma's smiling nod toward her unfailing tin full of icebox cookies. I still added their names to the family prayer Momma taught us. Whispering their names, my hands flattened together in the dark, I felt sure they were praying my name too.

⌒ ⌒

I was so happy to be upstairs. Yvonne would come from her dorm across the hall to tuck me in, half an hour before her own bedtime, always adding a polite "good night, Jane" to my doll friend. I wasn't afraid anymore in this large dormitory with fifteen beds row on row. I felt more anonymous, and comforted by being near Yvonne at last.

Then one spring night, loud bells interrupted my deep sleep. Adult arms grabbed me, carried me swiftly to an opening in the wall, and pushed me in, feet first. I felt myself circling in a closed tube, holding my breath, shivering in my pushed-up gown. Suddenly, pitch darkness gave way to moonlight, and hands caught me as I emerged from the spiral fire chute. The hands set me aside quickly to reach out for the next child, and I was left to stagger over to other white-clad figures huddled a few feet away. I felt faint, then Yvonne was there, talking, holding me up, upset that she hadn't warned me, mad at "those stupid poopheads" for not having my first fire drill in the daytime, as hers had been. For the next drill, and for all the rest of them, Yvonne defied the rules to dash across the hall at the first bell and run for the chute. When I completed my swift descent, she was there waiting behind the designated catcher.

"Here I am, Patty." And she led me away on my unsteady legs to the cool, damp grass.

When the days lengthened and we shed our coats, we made friends with the metal serpent. We climbed up its insides from ground level as far as we could, turned awkwardly in its grudging space, and slid down on our own terms.

⌒ ⌒

One day I ran to Yvonne's dormitory, terrified and shaking. The weekly head check had turned up lice in my hair.

"Gather your hat, scarf, brush, and comb quickly, Patty," the matron had said, "and report to the laundry building."

From stories we'd heard, we knew they would strip my clothes and pour kerosene on my scalp, then wrap my head in a towel and send me to the attic. There I would stay, sleeping on a thin washable mattress, until the parasites were gone.

Yvonne turned pale when I blubbered my instructions.

"How did you get 'em to let you come here?" she asked. She was always intrigued by successful excuses and stored the good ones for future use.

"I said I left my hairbrush in here." My stamping foot tried to bring her back to my problem.

Yvonne looked at my trembling chin and hesitated for a moment, weighing her options. Then she grabbed her brush from its spot in her neat locker, pulled it through my flyaway hair, and then through her own soft curls. She grabbed her hat and scarf from their hook and led me to the laundry building.

"I used my sister's brush," she explained to the surprised matron, who saw Yvonne's firm grip on my hand and didn't even check her disheveled curls.

Moments later we stood naked, with our heads hanging over the laundry tubs. We held our noses and squeezed our eyes shut against the foul kerosene. Through my nausea, I heard pitiful yelps alongside me—more like a wounded animal than like my sister, who usually cried softly.

While we climbed to the attic above our dormitories, gowned and humbled, Yvonne said, in her understated way, "I hope I never have to go through that again."

As it happened, I would not have been alone. Three other somber girls from my dorm arrived to share the delousing ritual. But it was Yvonne who sneaked bravely down the stairs late at night (saying, "What else can they do to me?") and brought back cookies, apples, and a fashion magazine—forbidden extras to lighten our exile.

When on the third day we descended to relate the horror story to our curious dormmates, we embellished on the previous tales. Our version claimed we had shared the cramped space with giant spiders and shadowy monsters and (as we warmed to our rapt audience) subsisted on bread and water. None of us mentioned the ice cream treats handed up to us after every lunch and supper. We sat there and devoured the attention, small martyrs, still stinking after several shampoos.

Kindergarten, in my old Minneapolis neighborhood, accepted any four-year-old who would turn five before January so I had qualified, barely, to enroll in Madison School a few weeks before our journey to Owatonna. Fortunately, the school building here included a kindergarten, so I was able to spend part of my long days in school.

And I welcomed the daily responsibilities of second-floor living. We had to make our own beds with square corners and perfectly smooth blankets. Here in the dormitories, for some fathomless reason, our pillows were not allowed under our heads; they spent the night in our lockers. But by day, they formed rounded mounds beneath the gray blankets, making our beds appear more hospitable than we knew them to be.

Each child had another task. For five-year-olds they were simple ones—setting or clearing tables, folding laundry, picking up the playroom at day's end. I asked for, and was granted, a job in the nursery building next to ours, helping the toddlers with their big bright puzzles and their marching games for a while before suppertime. "Guess what, Duaney? I get to see you every day!" As hard as this transplanting was, we three had common roots. Now I could spend more time with both my sister and my brother.

"Sis-e-e-e!" he'd squeal. He threw his pudgy weight into my arms as I sat on the floor, knocking me backwards as I held him tight. It was a dream come true.

It may have been there that I contracted tuberculosis. They said it was a mild case and recorded that I probably brought it with me from my birth home, although my admission X rays showed clear lungs and my Mantoux test had been negative.

The feared disease required isolation, and therefore an abrupt, no-hugs departure from Owatonna. I was whisked directly from our medical building into a big white vehicle. While a nurse bent over me, tucking a cool sheet around my prickly-hot body, I studied her starched cap and tried to complete half-questions: "Where are—? What is—?" until I slid into sleep. When I awoke, two white-clad men were lifting my stretcher off the van's platform. The brick building they carried me into was lower, lighter colored, and slightly friendlier looking than Owatonna's administration building—more like the hospital in our old neighborhood.

Treatment included a balanced diet, total bed rest, and regular sunlamp treatments. I was fortunate that, at this facility, heliotherapy had replaced the fresh air faddism of the 1920s, which forced patients, clad only in diaperlike "drapes," outside despite extremes of heat and cold, and sometimes led to pneumonia.

I was back in a crib, albeit a bigger one, that became my playpen by day. Every staff member I badgered with questions about my siblings assured me that my separation from them was temporary and vital for their protection.

Without visitors, I felt cut off from any existence of my own. I watched the nurses come and go and tried to imagine them at home, putting on real clothes, gathering flowers from their gardens. My active life had become a spectator sport.

At first the drugs kept me lethargic, but one day I asked, "Where is my Jane Withers doll?"

"If they bring the doll here," said the nurse, "it will be contaminated, and you won't be able to take it with you when you leave the sanitorium."

Her last word shocked me. God, I thought this was a hospital! Weren't sanitoriums where crazy people went? Then I decided it didn't really matter if I couldn't even have Jane. I had heard someone here say that tuberculosis could kill a person. If it didn't, I was sure this loneliness and monotony would.

chapter three

Foster Family

When I left the sanitorium, after four months of isolation from all but medical personnel and other tubercular children, they gave Jane back to me.

Through a battery of physical tests, the doctors had determined I was no longer contagious. It was common for TB patients to lose weight dramatically, but it was not so with my mild case, discovered in its earliest stages with a routine six-month Mantoux test. My face was even rounder than before, from inactivity and the prescribed high-calorie diet. I felt slower, restrained by invisible bonds.

My examiners seemed genuinely puzzled by my mental and psychological test results. In their minds, my ability didn't jibe with my reticent, almost guarded demeanor. Privately, I believed they'd understand better if they asked the right questions. Or better yet, if they let me ask some, and provided honest answers.

How could I respond to "What games do you like to play, Patricia?" when I didn't know if I'd ever see my family again? What difference did it make what my favorite color was when my choices were usually white or gray? Why should I tell them what my favorite foods were when I expected no choice at all?

Eventually, the anonymous adults who controlled my life decided I would need more careful supervision and tranquility than Owatonna could provide. This time, I would be uprooted all by myself and delivered to a family in a small town near Owatonna. This town, Faribault, was named for the fur trader who founded it and was known for its "Faribo" wool blankets.

The pair of proper state agents in a black sedan who escorted me to this town were generous with stories of its history and commerce, but stingy with information about my future.

No one explained to me what "foster" meant, but at age five and a half, I understood the word *home*. Because the adults in this foster home were to take care of me, and I was asked to call them Mom and Dad as the two other children did, I believed Mr. and Mrs. Franklin were my new parents, Bud and Sis my new brother and sister.

I was given a small neat room of my own, with blue and white striped wallpaper and a blue chenille bedspread. A place at the table was assigned to me—next to Sis, across from Bud. The dishes they used, I saw with a mixture of comfort and sadness, were the same ivy pattern as Grandma's.

I'd been allowed a short visit with Yvonne after my discharge from the sanitorium. At first, I thought my heart would stop every time I remembered Yvonne's screams when they pulled me away from her after that brief reunion in the reception room at Owatonna. And they wouldn't let me see my brother. I missed the feel of sweet Duane's fat fingers reaching for my face.

With only my doll Jane for company at night, I'd lie awake and think about my bed on the second floor. A yearning, sharp and painful, filled the spare length of me. I longed for Yvonne's soft voice, higher than mine but with that same lisp, singing one of the few songs she knew while she tucked me in so tight I couldn't move.

But it was Daddy who seemed sometimes to be there with me in the dark room, telling me not to be afraid, calming my pounding heart until I could fall asleep.

⌒ ⌒

I guessed quickly that Bud and Sis were born to this family; in some matters they were treated differently. Then I learned that Bud's given name, Walter, was the same as his father's. Sis got her nickname when three-year-old Bud couldn't pronounce Phyllis, so he mooshed it into something like Fhi-sis.

Walter Sr. went to work in a suit. His job had something to do with numbers, but he never discussed it at home. He believed it was incomprehensible to all of us, and so a waste of words.

Big and gruff, he subscribed easily to his wife's submissiveness. He'd play ball or checkers with Bud, take him fishing or to the hardware store. For Sis and me, he had questions about schoolwork or a pat on the head with compliments on our appearance. Occasionally he'd let us coax him into taking us out for ice cream (our coy, teasing approach worked best), and his wife would put on her straw hat and join us.

Beneath her hat, Mrs. Franklin's face wore a startled expression. Evangeline (no one attempted to shorten it) was aptly named. She peppered her conversations with biblical admonitions, not always relevant.

"The Lord loves a cheerful giver," she'd say in a chirpy tone at the slightest evidence of Sis's selfish instincts.

"Man shall not live by bread alone," she'd say seriously, sliding my glass of milk closer and giving a new interpretation to Matthew's words.

She was perpetually in motion and tended to all our physical comforts efficiently, but she seemed unwilling, or unable, to invest emotional warmth. Years later, a pastor I knew would describe Evangeline well: "Some people," he said, "are so heaven-centered they have trouble getting down to earth."

Sometimes, though, as she fussed with Sis's hair, a faint wistful smile would flit across her face, like a submerged desire trying to surface.

She didn't believe in corporal punishment; instead we girls would be required to read a Bible verse she chose ("Pride goeth before a fall" or "A soft answer turns away wrath"—she was partial to Proverbs), then reflect on our sin and ask God's forgiveness.

As for Bud, she seemed to have no idea how to relate to him. His punishments, permission for activities, attention were all left to his father. Her responsibility was limited to getting him to their Episcopal church on Sunday, in his white shirt and brown knickers, his unruly hair slicked back. He'd sit solemnly beside his mother while Sis and I, hatted and gloved, squirmed on her other side. When she shushed us, I'd watch the veil on her black Sunday cloche puff away from her pursed mouth.

Mr. Franklin always had "other important things to do" on Sunday mornings. Even as I called them Mom and Dad, they remained in my mind Mr. and Mrs. Franklin, as most other people addressed them. To me, dads were men who teased you affectionately, and moms held you when you hurt.

Sis, age eight like Yvonne, was prim but cheerful. She let me sit beside her at the piano while she demonstrated the progress from her last lesson.

Sis had an imaginary friend; her name was Eve. Eve was not a playmate but an adviser and sometimes a scapegoat. Sis asked Eve's advice about everything from her hairdo to her homework.

"And don't tell me Bible verses," Sis would say to her in an imploring tone, "just tell me!" Once, when Sis was scolded for picking a neighbor's flowers, she told me, "Eve did it." I pointed out that I'd seen Sis with the bouquet, and she said, bristling, "But Eve did it, because she didn't tell me I shouldn't."

Few things exasperated Sis's mother as much as these end runs around her moral certitudes. Mrs. Franklin finally forbade any mention of Eve (although she failed to find a verse to justify banning the invisible lodger). But I would hear Sis whispering to Eve at night in her room next to mine, after Mrs. Franklin had listened, kneeling, to Sis's prayers and then quietly left the room.

Bud was mean to me sometimes, yet he seemed to prefer my company to that of his delicate, fussy sister. I looked up to him because I hadn't known any boys well who were as old as eleven. He taught me card games and gave me some of his marbles, surprised at how well I could shoot. I kept them, with my rubber ball and set of jacks, in a box I'd kept from the animal crackers they gave me the day I arrived at their shuttered and shaded house.

A weeping willow stood just where a hill behind the house met the smooth sweep of lawn. The space between its trunk and drooping branches provided a summer hiding place, a quiet retreat where I could write in my tablet or draw pictures while patches of sunlight danced on the page. I could talk to Jane there too, about Yvonne and Duane, because she was the only one here who had known them.

School began—first grade. I was eager to learn to read, and it came easily. I barely paused at the simple books that Sis kept stacked on her desk. Soon I was raiding Bud's bookshelves, slowly and phonetically devouring *Tom Sawyer* and *Swiss Family Robinson* and other adventures chosen for Bud by the unadventurous Mr. Franklin.

Christmas was a wonder of lights, presents, and food. Even my sixth birthday brought a whole cake, a pickup-sticks game in a narrow can, and three pretty underpants, each sprinkled with pink, blue, or yellow flowers.

One midwinter afternoon I lay reading, and Sis was sliding alone (or more likely with Eve) behind the house. One of them crashed Sis's sled into a tree. Mrs. F., in a panic, left Bud in charge while she hustled her teary and frightened daughter off to their doctor. When they returned, Sis proudly displayed her splinted and bandaged wrist.

But in the meantime, Bud had shattered the fragile comfort I'd begun to feel. With threats of getting me turned out into the dark of night ("with owls and bats and fierce alley cats"), he'd forced his hands up my dress, down my flowered pants. This time, as I hovered near the ceiling, I felt as if Daddy held me there, smiling, waiting for his good night kiss.

Through the next couple of months, I managed to avoid being alone with Bud, mainly by becoming Sis's shadow. She hated cards and

marbles, and would only play house and "dress-up." She avoided
dirty hands and clothes as carefully as I avoided dirty Bud.

Sis had a piano lesson after school one day a week. I could no
longer go on home by myself, in case Bud was there alone. I waited
on the steps outside the piano teacher's house, cold even in my wool
coat, leggings, and a heavy stocking cap and mittens handed down
from Sis. One day the piano teacher caught sight of me through the
window as I jumped up and down to keep warm.

"Why didn't you tell me your little sister was out there?" she
asked. She frowned at Sis and hurried me inside. For once Sis was
silent, but her cheeks burned red. After that, I waited in the kitchen
and sipped warm Ovaltine with a big marshmallow slowly dissolving
on top.

Sis stopped showing me the piano pieces she'd learned. She knew
I'd heard them many times before, heard her teacher say patiently,
"No, dear, it's still not right." Sis hated being corrected, especially
in front of me.

There had always been a few "bad boys" on the playground who
would try out their vulgar words and crude touching on any girl
whose guard was down. But I never dreamed that Bud, my tall
friend, my game partner, would make me a victim of his curiosity.
Whenever Bud got near me now, he punched or pinched. His parents
seemed to notice only when I hit back. He'd leer at me across the
table through narrowed eyes. Even when I avoided looking back, I
could feel his cold stare in my churning stomach.

One afternoon he pinned me down in his room, feigning anger
over a book I'd just returned. When he tried to force my legs apart,
I bit the arm that lay like a heavy bar across my face. His yelp brought
his mother on the run. It was a good bite, a two-Bible-verse one, but
this time my penance was not the end of it.

It was clear that Mrs. Franklin was disturbed, and probably suspicious. Now she watched every exchange between Bud and me out of
the corner of her eye. I believe she identified the undercurrent cor-
rectly, yet avoided a confrontation with her son.

My welcome was definitely eroding. Unable to sleep in my bedroom in the quiet house, I would float to the ceiling and look down

at Patty in her bed, a phenomenon that seemed less absurd to me than the rest of my topsy-turvy world.

I wrote poems in my tablet:

> When I fly
> I am part of the sky.
> Like a bird, they can't touch me if I don't touch the floor
> They can only watch me soar.

As insecure as I felt (they found me sleepwalking on a few occasions), I was wholly unprepared when the black sedan arrived early one morning.

There were no explanations, just brief stiff good-byes. Then Jane and me, in the back seat alone, with a few shopping bags holding my belongings. Tears streamed down my face and neck, soaking the collar of my dress. Bitter desolate tears of defeat, rejection, and humiliation. But with each sob I felt the terrible tension of the past weeks draining away. When the flood stopped, I felt resigned, almost peaceful. But so cold, tired. I put my head down on the seat. I could still remember the words: He restores my soul, thy rod and thy staff, they comfort me.

chapter

four

Foster Group Home

I awoke when the car stopped and the solemn woman stepped from the front seat. Somehow, I already knew they weren't taking me back to Owatonna, to my own sister and brother. Not to Minneapolis and Momma either.

"I'll be back soon," she told the driver, who seemed nervous. He had glanced anxiously at me a few times without speaking. In his mirror, I saw his eyes follow me while I examined my tender right cheek. It carried an imprint from the Ford's woven straw seat covers.

The woman reappeared after a few minutes. "Let's see if we can make you presentable," she said, and she straightened my damp collar and pulled a comb through my hair.

The house she led me and Jane toward was older and bigger than the Franklins', and it had no immediate neighbors. I tried to avoid the cracks on the sidewalk while we squeezed around shrubbery that looked unruly compared to the Franklins' clipped hedges.

Inside, several children stared at my swollen face. There were seven or eight of them, all fosterlings like me, I was sure. "Welcome, Patty. I'm Miss Clara.'' The woman beamed and laid a fat hand on my shoulder as she spoke. ''What a sweet, pretty girl,'' she said, ignoring my red puffy sullen face. ''I'll be taking care of you from now on.''

Miss Clara's tiny nose barely provided a perch for her glasses. Tight brown curls ringed her pale, pudgy face. One curl hung down her forehead above crimson cheeks and lips. When she pointed at something, as she often did, her upper arm jiggled in her sleeveless housedress. The other kids seemed to like her, and to vie for her attention. Well, let them, I thought; I would not be fooled again.

I'd always had a hard time throwing anything away, maybe because I traveled light as it was. But now I tossed the animal cracker box and Bud's marbles in the garbage can. I kept my ball and jacks and the pick-up sticks, deciding I'd need some things I could play with all by myself.

At age six and a half, I was determined to become emotionally independent and trust no one but me. I found ways to be alone whenever possible and turned belligerent when I had to share my space. Soon I had alienated everyone in the house. Everyone except Sally the giggler.

Sally was a tiny girl, my age but even smaller than I, with reddish braids and more freckles than I'd seen before. She found me on my first day at Miss Clara's house, in the large old bathroom, looking for a lever on the toilet. She giggled and pulled the chain alongside the wall, and giggled again at my astonishment when it flushed. Even our old apartment in Minneapolis had modern plumbing by comparison.

I kept telling her to leave me alone. Still, she'd sneak up behind me and put her cold hands over my eyes.

''Guess who-o?'' she'd ask, and her high-pitched laugh provided the instant answer. Or she'd stick a raisin ''curl'' on her forehead, push her nose up with her finger, puff out her cheeks, and mimic Miss Clara's slow shuffle.

I tried to fight it, but something deep inside me, something I thought was safely corked and sealed, bubbled high and spilled over, turning up the corners of my mouth, lighting my eyes. Then Sally would stand, hands on hips, and bat her eyes at me, trying to force my total surrender.

Meanwhile, I was getting nowhere in my attempt to reform a timid girl named Olivia (an attempt undertaken simply because I disliked timidity). You could tell the shy ones because they tended to move their widened eyes without moving their heads. Often, they held on to something, if only their clothes or their own hands.

"Oogie," as other children called her, upset me because she wouldn't stick up for herself. I'd find her weeping in a corner, cowed by someone's slight or scorn, her eggshell complexion all red-blotched. I tried to coach her in survival tactics that were so against her nature they only made her more fearful.

One day, after Sally witnessed my failure, she drew Olivia to the middle of the playroom and there engaged her in pure nonsense. They braided each other's bangs, then Olivia mirrored Sally's funny faces. Other girls gathered to watch the show, eager to join the games that already included a happily grinning Olivia at center stage.

For solitude, I discovered a tree that sheltered a corner of the overgrown back yard. Its strong limbs formed a perch that held me securely, six feet above the ground, while I wrote in my tablet:

> The tree and me
> Both alive and free
> Need sunlight, water, food and air
> And for a while, some tender care.
> God sends golden rays
> To light our days
> Then rain, seeds, and sparkling air
> And human hearts to show his care.
> The gentle hearts are there
> Somewhere.

One day, two young women wearing sundresses came and took all the children to the nearest town in two square black cars. Young female drivers were a novelty to me. I noticed how capable they looked behind the big steering wheels.

When we parked, I saw signs that told me we were in the town of Owatonna. In the five- and ten-cent store, with its soda fountain along one side, we each had a glass of 7UP. It was my very first one.

Peering through the bottom of my glass, I tried to figure out why they called it that. The bubbles went up all right, but there were more than seven of them.

Sally, by my side as usual, said it tickled her nose, and emphasized by tickling mine with her straw. Her demonstrative ways were so opposite from my attempted stoicism, I wondered why she bothered with me. Was I a challenge for her? Or did she see through my tough veneer? How could any child who had gotten to this place be so cheerful?

"Now you may each pick out a small toy," said sundress when we'd drained our soda pop. I found some wondrous glass balls that snowed inside when you tipped them upside down. I took my time deciding between two of them. Staring at one with a pink ballerina, I admired her tutu—layers of real lace—and wondered how they got her inside the seamlessly closed ball. The other ball held a little house and snowman that looked more natural in the sparkly blizzard.

I felt a hand on my shoulder. "Sorry, Patty, those cost too much money." So I chose a plastic puzzle with tiny lead balls that would roll into shallow holes if you moved it just right. Sally got a paddle and a rubber ball joined by a rubber string. The first time I tried to bounce the ball on the paddle I hit my forehead with the ball, and Sally giggled hysterically.

On our way back to the cars, we stopped at Candy Kitchen. We had our choice of a caramel or a piece of fudge. I tied my wrapped caramel into the embroidered handkerchief Grandma had sent me and tucked the bundle into the patch pocket of my skirt. It would be my special treat for another day. This day was already sweet enough.

Riding home, Sally stood behind our driver, whose long shiny hair fell softly down past the top of her sundress. Sally stroked the young woman's hair almost reverently. From my place next to her in the back seat, I saw Sally's chin quiver, heard a shuddered sigh, and quickly turned away. I didn't want to know if she had hidden demons too.

☞ ☜

The morning that Sally didn't come down for breakfast, I asked Miss Clara (to whom I rarely spoke directly), "Where is Sally?"

"We sent her to the hospital last night," she said.

"Is it TB?" I wanted to know.

"No, Patty, they think it's pneumonia." Relieved that it wasn't the one that I knew could kill you, I asked if they could take my plastic puzzle to her.

"Not right now, dear," she said, as she dabbed a handkerchief between her eyes and her glasses. Her kind words surprised me. Her tone with me, a definite problem child, was usually sharp with irritation. When Sally hadn't returned after a few days, I became obsessed with worry. Tomorrow was the first day of school. She'd been so excited about starting second grade. Where was she? And her personal things had disappeared too!

I felt too sick and anxious to face school the next morning. After the other children left, Miss Clara, already angry at me for postponing her first day without kids, discovered I had wet the bed during the night. She flew into a rage and pushed my face into the wet sheet. I'd never seen her so vicious.

"It should have been you," she said, her voice tight, "instead of Sally!"

"What do you mean?" I sputtered, and broke away from her grip. "Never mind," she said firmly. Suddenly calmer, she left the bedroom. I stood there, trying to swallow.

I found her later at the kitchen table in her housedress and slippers, smoking, a half bottle of beer next to her chubby hand. I had to know.

"What about Sally?" I asked. A bitter taste rose in my throat.

"I told you, never mind," she answered primly.

"You're a mean old shitty pig!" I was frustrated and scared. She lunged out of her chair, gripped my arm, and pulled me to the sink. She seized a handful of my hair, yanked my head back, and forced a corner of the Fels Naptha soap bar into my mouth.

"We'll just clean up your filthy mouth," she said in a loud staccato. I believed she had turned into the wicked witch from *Snow White* right before my eyes.

Gagging, I kicked back into her puffy ankle as hard as I could. She screamed, grabbed her cigarette off the table, and tried to press it to my cheek. I whipped my head away, but the glowing ash brushed across my cheekbone.

I tried not to faint, and threw up instead. She reached for a dish towel, twisted it into a rope, and tied my wrists tightly together. She dragged me across the room (I didn't know she was so strong) and threw me into the pantry, a tall shallow closet with shelves that filled the top half. My arm scraped against a step stool as she closed and latched the door.

The vomit smell from my dress filled the cramped space. Blood beaded up on my arm. Sobbing, I started to pound on the door with my bound fists, but then decided I might be better off where I was. Maybe I would just die right here. Then would I go wherever Sally was?

I crouched low and tried to see out the narrow vents that allowed me some faint light. Finally, with the damp dish towel against my cheek burn, I fell asleep. Before the other children returned from school, Miss Clara pulled me from the closet and sent me to the bathroom to bathe and change to pajamas. She led me upstairs to a clean bed, left water and supper on the night table, and belatedly smeared Vaseline on my cheek, acting as though nothing had happened. I heard the children bounding through the house and Miss Clara, on the stairs, telling them not to disturb me.

The next day, although I was still shaky and distraught, I didn't even consider staying home. I chose the dress with three-quarter-length sleeves to cover my scratched arm. At school, my new teacher asked about the ugly raw mark on my face. Because it still hurt, I said boldly, "Miss Clara burned me."

"I'm sure it was an accident," she said matter-of-factly.

"It wasn't," I said coldly.

No one ever talked to me about it again, just as they didn't talk about Sally. But a few days later, a woman I'd never seen was waiting for me after school. She had a small canvas bag filled with my things.

chapter five

Back to Owatonna

After my second experience with foster care, another pair of state agents delivered me back to Owatonna's state school.

Yvonne was overjoyed to see me, after more than a year. Her hug lifted my feet off the floor. "Oh, honey, honey," she cried, pressing her wet cheek against mine. And she was surprised how much I had changed.

"What's the matter, Pattycake?" she asked when I wiggled away from her smothering kisses. She sounded like Momma. I couldn't explain that I was afraid to get close, even to her, again.

They had told me that Duane was gone now, adopted, out of our lives forever.

"When did they take Duaney away?" I asked Yvonne.

"Right after you left—it was just before my birthday," she said, sobbing harder now. "But they said I couldn't t-tell you when you came here that day, after the hospital."

She told me every detail of the morning they woke her to say good-bye to him. About his big smile, until her scream—when they told her—frightened him. She had obviously replayed the scene in her head many times.

"Do you know where he went?" I asked.

"I heard them say 'up north' somewhere—on a f-farm, I think."

She could barely get the words out. I tried to distance myself from the experience that hurt her so, as if she were speaking of someone else, not my own soft little brother. But I couldn't flatten out the sharp cutting edges inside. I was certain I'd never be happy again.

⌒ ⌒

In the tall cupboard full of toys that the girls in our building shared at playtime, there was a small broom and dustpan. I'd sweep the whole activity area, forcing the other girls to move their toys or have them covered with dust.

"Stop it!" they'd say indignantly, dragging their doll blankets and checkerboards from the path of my charging broom. But they were merely motherless dwarfs, and I was Snow White, in charge of keeping this cottage clean. It was my purpose for being here. Identifying with the fairy tale made my haphazard life feel more guided, as if someday a happier plot would be played out for me, too.

In school, my teacher told us a legend about traveling Scandinavian oak trees. They grew far in the north when it was still warm there, but then, as if warned of the eventual change of climate, they began producing acorns only on the south side of the tree, so that they gradually traveled southward. Millions of years later, they reached Spain, where, in a hospitable place, they resumed normal propagation.

I thought about that story for weeks. After chapel service, I asked the minister if the Bible told about it. He listened patiently, then laughed and said, "Now where did you hear a story like that?"

I wanted the story to be about God. If it was about nature, it might only apply to trees. For a child in this place, encouraged to make no demands, entertain no hopes, it would be reassuring to feel as well protected as those oaks. (Weird, I thought, to be jealous of a tree.) Looking back, I wonder if the real message of the traveling oaks was this: God's will unchanged by mortals. That is, no person moved the acorns back to the north side of the trees. Could God care for humans as perfectly, if only we didn't continually thwart the divine plan? Gradually, with the natural resilience that must be God's gift to children, I felt the wound-up tightness in my chest ease a little, allowed my thoughts to turn outward.

I liked learning new things. My second grade classes met in the classroom building on the state school campus, toward the back of the complex. Next to it, a separate gymnasium with a pool was used for physical education. Gender-segregated team sports were played on the ball fields. For boys, boxing was mandatory, and a showcase in the administration building displayed many Golden Glove trophies.

The older children's curriculum leaned heavily toward vocational training. Already, Yvonne took cooking and sewing. By sixth grade, the girls also were taught child tending and professional baking, and the boys learned about plants, animals, and machinery. For high school, the children were enrolled in the public school system in Owatonna, the boys hauled in trucks, the girls in a rickety bus, all of them wearing clunky brown leather oxfords donated by a well-meaning Minnesota shoe manufacturing company.

"Hey, mongrel," the town kids would jeer, "where can I get some clodhoppers like that?"

"Don't get stuck in the mud. You'll never get out!"

We heard stories from the older kids of teasing and torment—yet most of the "town kids" knew better than to risk a fist fight.

Children could live at the state school until they turned eighteen and found employment. Boys and girls ages fifteen to eighteen rose at four in the morning to work in the barns or bakery. Fourteen-year-olds frequently were sent to a farm or home in the surrounding rural community to work as hired hands or housekeepers in return for room and board. This arrangement was accurately called "indenture."

We heard, from young serfs who had been returned to the school and now waited on our tables, woeful stories about adult overseers who refused to send them to school or denied them the freedoms given the natural-born children in the home. Several of the girls bore children fathered by their foster fathers or brothers. After hearing those accounts, we felt fortunate to remain in the institution.

I spent my free school hour each day in the library; its shelves were full of escape from the confinement of my small world.

No one here was assigned to answer all my burning questions, nor could I find volunteers patient enough to endure my ceaseless curiosity for long. If I ever raised children, I vowed, I would answer their every "But *why?*" For who could know which question was truly important, which might lead to a whopping discovery? To a shoelace that stayed tied—or a cure for pneumonia?

I sought answers in the magic pages of books. Where did the trains, whistling through this town on their urgent timetable, end up, anyway? And what about the airplanes that flew uncommonly overhead, causing everyone to squint skyward? (I hopefully imagined each plane to be piloted by Amelia Earhart, returning alive and safe after all.)

And what about "all the ships at sea" that Walter Winchell greeted so inclusively when he opened his radio broadcasts? His words were as clipped as the teletype that clicked in the background. "Good evening, Mr. and Mrs. North and South America, and all the ships at sea. Let's go to press!" he'd say. He tried to make his thin voice sound dramatic while he rapidly emptied his bag of celebrity secrets.

Soon the books told me far more about New Zealand and Bali than I knew about Owatonna. I could identify mineral rocks and shells that waited for me on distant hillsides and shores I planned to visit one day.

Something worried me. What if a person's brain contained only so much wire or whatever held all this knowledge inside our heads? And, when it was full, we couldn't learn anymore? Maybe I should be careful, not remember the boring stuff, save room for all that was surprising and wonderful. After all, there were still those hundreds of books in the adult section. (Years later, a teacher would say of me, "She's smart, but she only applies herself to things that interest her.")

Our teacher read to us every day—A. A. Milne. I thought I had outgrown Christopher Robin, not learning until later that I never would, but I loved to listen to Miss O'Leary's hushed voice and watch her pale eyelids and soft shoulders relax with the pleasure of entering Pooh's world.

⌐ ⌐

On Wednesday evenings, the staff showed movies in the auditorium, which was also used then for Sunday chapel and for school plays and assemblies. We sat on the floor, legs crossed, chins tilted up to a screen that pulled down from the ceiling, so that the price of this diversion was a stiff neck.

Only those children who had behaved during the past week were allowed. Any act of misbehavior, or an accident such as spilling on the tablecloth, earned a check mark on a child's weekly chart. Five check marks meant no movie. As often as not, I was barred, or Yvonne had lost her privilege, usually by defending me physically or finishing my meal (against the rules). It wasn't that I was a finicky eater; my sensitive stomach rebelled no matter what the menu if I entered a dining room with mingled smells of foods, wet mittens, and disinfectant.

When both of us managed to get passes for the movie, Yvonne would grab a spot at the back where she could sit against the wall. When my group entered, I'd scramble to the far side of the room, away from the watchful eyes of the matrons whose chairs guarded the doors. After the room was darkened, I'd gradually scoot back until I reached Yvonne, where I would sit between her raised knees and lean my head against her shoulder. As soon as "The End" appeared on the screen, the children would stand, eager to ease their cramped legs. Small and quick, I'd slip unnoticed back to my place before the eyes of the sentinels could adjust to the light.

But I felt freer, less pressured, in the open air. It was fall, always my favorite season. I loved the bite in the air that turned my cheeks pink, and the smell of burning leaves. This time, the grass fires didn't get out of hand as they had two years ago, causing one of the barns to burn on the night we arrived. Large trees canopied the grounds behind our brick building. We raked leaves into deep piles and jumped into them from a low toolshed. They smelled damp and dusty, and crackled around us.

The playground's tall swings made me motion sick. I liked the teeter-totter, until a nervous girl named Gloria slid off her lowered perch, letting me crash on the hard ground. I made sure Gloria felt the hard ground too, but it cost me a whole day of outdoor play. I would have preferred the next level of punishment—hard whacks with a radiator brush.

There was a wonderful, huge piece of equipment with slides and rings. I liked its horizontal bars best (they were called "turning poles" then). I swung on them like a monkey; I could hang by my knees and somersault off better than the big kids. When I sat on the highest bar, I felt omnipotent. I was the beloved queen, bestowing favors on all my subjects. One day I would wave my stick "wand" and abolish jails; the next day I might populate an entire town with mirthful Sallys.

The gym and playground shared a circular road with the laundry and carpenter shop. Behind them were the farm buildings—barn, stable, chicken coops—and, by this time, more than two hundred acres of pasture and farmland where much of the food was grown to feed the staff and children. Over the eighty-three-year history of that institution, from 1887 to 1970, there would be more than twenty thousand children. (After 1945, the facility served educable mentally retarded children before becoming, in 1974, the West Hills complex of city-administered services.)

South, by a hill, stood a greenhouse where hundreds of plants were nurtured, a large root cellar for vegetable storage, and a machine shop. The imposing castlelike administration building was solidly built of red brick and Kasota limestone. Its main floor held separate dining rooms for boys, girls, and staff, and also a kitchen, offices, and a reception room where parents who remained deferential to the administrators were granted occasional visits with their children, until the children were placed with other families.

The basement below the administration building housed a barber shop, a bakery, a butcher shop, walk-in freezers, a shoe repair shop, and a room where milk was pasteurized. The second floor accommodated the supplies and equipment used by the school's seamstresses.

Trees in the orchard near the admissions building were heavy now with green apples. Ignoring staff warnings, I ate ten of them one day and was punished with an incredible stomachache.

The boys would throw apples to the transient men who hung from the freight trains. The boxcars crawled slowly behind the farm buildings and the small, gently tended cemetery half filled with little white crosses.

Not all the young wards of the state welcomed fall as I did. Harvest time meant long days for many scrawny boys, lifting half their weight in burlap bags full of vegetables. Even more hapless were those lads assigned to clear out the root cellar, remove rotten vegetables from the dark smelly space, and scrub it for the newly harvested crop.

Snowfall brought partial relief from chores. But on snowy mornings, the maintenance supervisor would rouse a team of boys before dawn so they could clear all the walks by breakfast time: ''Awright, everybody up. Daylight in the swamps. Let's go!'' These boys would have little trouble adjusting to army life later. Other children scrubbed the tile dining hall floor three times a day, battling against the tracked slush and sticky spills of the hungry herd.

Two years earlier, during our first Christmas season in Owatonna, Yvonne and I had each received a small box in the mail: assorted hard candy—peppermint sticks, root beer barrels, lemon balls—and a few whips of licorice. The card bore a Bible verse and the name of our Minneapolis Sunday school teacher, Esther Jenson. I couldn't believe she would spend her time and money on us; we weren't even in her family. And we didn't have the means to thank her. But we doled the candy out to ourselves sparingly over several days and traded favorite pieces.

Now the candy arrived again, to our delight, and Yvonne remembered to tell me that the boxes were delivered last year too, when I was with the Franklins. Some staff people had opened and divided mine, although they surely knew how to find me. I wondered why they could steal my present and not go to jail, as Daddy had when he stole something. It was my first lesson in unequal justice.

⸙ ⸙

Rehearsals for our Christmas play began. I would be one of the wooden toy soldiers, dancing stiff-legged in our simplified version of *The Nutcracker*.

Just as practice ended one day, Momma arrived alone with presents—hat, mittens, and a book for each of us. Her brown hair, stringy the last time I saw her, was softly curled. Her manner, too, was different from the tender Momma of our last visit. That time, after our long separation, she had cuddled me on her lap, almost moaning her words: "You're back—oh, God, you're really here." Now she seemed to be guarding herself from us—from me especially.

"Who drove you here?" Yvonne asked, knowing Momma didn't drive.

"Well, um-m, he's waiting in the car."

I told myself I didn't care. But my sister always needed to find the sore spots and then try to heal them.

"When is Daddy getting out?" Yvonne blurted the words boldly.

Momma seemed startled. "Not for a while." Then, anticipating Yvonne's next question, she said, "Howard is a friend who drives me sometimes." She averted her eyes for a silent moment before asking about our play. We demonstrated our steps for her. She didn't know if she could return for the performance, but she would try. She stood to leave.

Suddenly I felt terrified that she would never return, that I wouldn't see her again. I had so many questions. I ran and grabbed her around the knees.

"Please, Patty," she said in a slow desperate tone. "It's hard enough to come here and not see Duane. Please don't make it harder." She hugged us, hard and quick, and then she was gone. Even her faint, familiar warm scent was erased by the cold draft that entered the room as she left.

I looked for her from the stage the night of the production but saw only a sea of coats topped with blurred faces. Afterwards, while we celebrated with nectar and cookies, I was told someone wanted to see me. Momma? Maybe even Daddy? But it was a man and his wife from Minneapolis. They were hoping to find, in this place, a child to adopt.

Mrs. Scott was dark and pretty. She talked softly and with dignity. She gave me a tiny doll in a white lacy dress, too fragile to play with—more like one for the shelf in Sis's room.

"I l-o-oved your pretty dancing," she said. "Such a dainty, pretty girl you are." I felt she was seeing someone I didn't even know.

I wanted them to leave so I could return to the party. When they did, the treats were being cleared, the decorations removed. Yvonne had held back, looking for me.

"Where did you go?" she asked anxiously.

"I had to talk to a man and lady who want to get a kid here," I said.

Yvonne's body tensed; she looked terrified. "You're going away—like Duane!" Her voice was shrill.

"No," I said. "I think they're looking at a lot of kids. They won't want me. I didn't even talk much."

Yvonne would not be consoled. She started to plan how we could run away.

"Kids do it all the time!"

"They always bring 'em back," I said. "Remember the Prentice twins?"

But she continued to plot our escape. "A fire drill," she said. "We'll keep our clothes on under our nightgowns."

"And go where?" I asked.

"If we bring lots of apples," she said, ignoring the fact that the trees were bare now, "the bums will help us get on the train."

It was Yvonne's habit, even in calmer times, to become highly emotional over gifts and festive moments, so much so that I wondered how she could possibly enjoy Christmas. She trembled at the first sight of our cottage's yule tree and stared wide-eyed at the holiday array of food, too excited to eat. Her shaking hands worked on the wrappings of her donated comb or socks until I'd grab the package and strip it in one motion.

This year, her third Owatonna Christmas, her paranoia about my possible adoption added another quivery layer of anxiety.

"That was my worst time," she told me again, "when you got sick and they took you away. And when you were better, I couldn't believe they took you again. Why do I always have to stay behind?" It was a long speech for my sister, who was usually succinct. She was right. We'd been through so much together; why should we be separated?

I wiped her tears and put my arms around her. "Maybe they just can't let you go because you're so special."

By the day of my seventh birthday, she didn't want me out of her sight. She stared coldly at every stranger, until she even had me jerking around to examine newcomers. But when six more weeks had passed, I was relieved, confident the dignified lady and her tall husband had forgotten all about me.

Then abruptly one morning our floor matron supervised my dressing and brought coats for Yvonne and me. Outside, in the quiet chill, she took a picture of us together.

''Give each other a nice hug now,'' she said, ''and say good-bye.''

chapter

six

Adoption

A steady February snowfall slowed our drive from Owatonna to
the northern edge of Minneapolis. I tried hard not to be carsick because I didn't know if it would make this Mom and Dad angry.

Mrs. Scott sat between her husband and me. Mr. Scott said little,
except to comment on driving conditions and the cost of the trip. He
sat far back in the seat, so that all I could see of him was the front
brim of his homburg hat, the bowl of his pipe, and long fingers grip-
ping the gearshift that rose tall from its floor mounting.

By now, at age seven, I'd gone from birth home to state school and
foster homes, so I knew that an adoptive home was meant to be permanent. I was afraid of another transplanting. This time I was torn
forever from the two precious children who shared my roots. Their
bright smiles had brought the only reliable comfort to my life.

Yvonne had promised, gulping sobs, to write and tell me everything, although neither of us knew whether it was allowed. Anyway,
it wouldn't be the same as hearing my sister's matter-of-fact voice
while her fingers brushed back my hair. Our brother Duane, not yet

three years old, might have already forgotten me, I realized with a deep ache.

". . . and your grade school is right across the street from our home," Mrs. Scott was saying sweetly. "There is a little playground too." Her voice and manner had, no doubt, impressed Her Majesty, Owatonna's refined head matron.

With my nose pressed against the sleeve of her fur jacket, in a losing effort to escape the pipe smoke, I stared fascinated at the fox pelt that circled her shoulders. It had beady eyes and a mouth that formed a clasp to hold its tail. I was still studying it curiously when the soft, soothing voice lulled me to sleep.

I had planned to stay awake, after hearing that Minneapolis was our destination, to watch for my block, the familiar park, our school and library. First we would come to the sign with a big arrow pointing down to advertise the grocery store below street level in a large brick building. To me, "Minneapolis" named this neighborhood and, further away, a hospital and Aunt Ruth's and Grandma's houses.

When we drove past these places, I would pay close attention and memorize the route from our apartment to the Scotts' house. (Hansel and Gretel's bread trick, even if I had some crumbs, wouldn't work in this snow.) I was sure I could find my way back.

When I did, Momma would be so glad to see me! She'd make some rice pudding with raisins in it, just for me, and I'd tell her everything I'd been holding inside. Then we'd plan together, there in the cinnamon-smelling kitchen, how to get Yvonne and Duane back with us, how to take care of each other until Daddy came home.

But now as I slept, my face against the unfamiliar fur, I dreamed my familiar dream. Leaves fell from a mammoth tree—large leaves like name tags cut from paper, in deep colors of copper, golden rust, maroon, and olive. Each bore the face of someone I loved. Hitting the ground, they would take a tantalizing bounce toward me, but when I tried to scoop them up, they slipped through the oval of my arms, just out of reach, and drifted from sight into a dense fog. I shouted to them, but my echo voice blew back in my face.

We stopped at a garage door in an alley behind a stucco house. For one sleepy moment, I was elated—Grandma and Grandpa's house!

But no, their house had windows across the back, overlooking their vegetable garden.

I stepped out of the car into a shivery wind in my short navy coat, a dark blue tam pulled over short straight hair. I was nearly knocked over by a bounding German shepherd.

"Duke!" called a boy's voice from the doorway, and the dog backed away. A tall boy of eleven stepped out and said "hi" with a shy, curious look.

Inside the house, the air felt oppressively warm, the walls close, in contrast to the large drafty rooms I'd left behind. And so quiet. My clatter-accustomed senses strained for the din of children's voices.

Patrick Scott stayed in the background, looking awkward and uncertain. His mother gave me a small purse with some change in it. "It's from Patrick," she said. "He saved his allowance for this present. Wasn't that wonderful of him?" I took advantage of the rawness of the situation and didn't answer. I wondered why he didn't give it to me himself, if he really wanted to be friends.

Mrs. Scott wanted to take my picture in front of the house. First she removed my tam (like Yvonne's red one, it was a gift from Momma's last visit) and replaced it with a pale blue angora cloche hat with matching gloves. On the front step, she handed me the miniature doll. I felt so clumsy holding her that I perched her on the doorknob, then stood miserably for the picture, thinking about my last photograph with Yvonne, early that morning.

The house was small, minuscule compared to the buildings that cast monolithic shadows over the grounds of the state school in Owatonna. There were two bedrooms with a bathroom in between along the north side of the east-facing house. A small living room, dining room, and kitchen lined up on the south side in between a front vestibule and a small enclosed back entryway.

I was to sleep in a youth bed, a single bed with rails halfway down the sides. Patrick had a double bed in the same crowded room, and a chest of drawers and night table. Mrs. Scott's things filled most of the long maple dresser. I could use the remaining third of that, and a small space in the closet. No matter. I had very little material baggage, and no drawers could hold the emotional kind.

Mr. Scott had finally removed his hat, and he was bald, except for some thin strands combed across the top of his head. His face was square and handsome like Patrick's, his voice low and deliberate. He sat in his velour chair in a corner of the living room. Alongside the deep chair, scaled to his six-foot, three-inch height, stood an end table with a leatherette center. It held a large ashtray, a pipe rack with three pipes, and a can of Prince Albert tobacco.

He listened attentively to commentator H. V. Kaltenborn's news program. I could hear, across crackling wires, Adolf Hitler's shrill, hysterical voice, building his tyranny of molded men. Although the war in Europe seemed distant to me, our American continent secure between the oceans, I was afraid of the small man with a square mustache and the same limp greasy hair as the Owatonna janitor.

Finally, Mr. Scott switched off the console radio and called me to his side for our first conversation. He held a pipe in one hand and a list in the other—things he wanted to tell me. First, I should call him and his wife Dad and Mother as Patrick did. Second, we would not talk about my "past" anymore; I was to forget all about that.

The imposed secrecy flooded over me in a wave of shame and confusion. I wanted to run and hide, but his intense blue eyes behind the bifocal lenses held me there. I felt his piercing look sever my roots cleanly and toss them into a void. He couldn't know what he was asking. Forget everyone I'd ever known? Pretend my life never happened?

"One more thing," he said solemnly. "There was a girl we knew named Donna Ruth." (Was? Like Sally?)

"Do you like that name?" It was the first question he'd asked me. I nodded my head dumbly, thinking, "What does it possibly matter whether I like it or not?"

"Good," he said, apparently satisfied, "then that will be your name from now on." How easily he threw my own name into the abyss too, and slammed and locked the iron lid.

⌐ ⌐

My name was the one thing I had assumed I could keep. It was an integral part of me, like my straight purposeful walk, like my earnest voice that struggled with pronunciation so that sometimes adults would listen hard, their faces drawn into a question, as if they wanted to help me. I had heard "Patty" whispered to me in the dark, and I had responded to it in classrooms. I had listened for it shyly when it was my turn for the happy birthday song. I had expected to hear it pronounced at my graduation and my wedding. Without it I felt naked and defenseless, a tree with no bark.

"Dear Father in heaven," I prayed that night, "the Duane I've been praying for might of had his name changed, so I'll just pray for my little brother and you'll know who I mean. And if you get any prayers for Patty Ann, please switch them to Donna Ruth."

I lay awake for a long time, startled by each chiming of the grandfather clock, wondering what could happen to me next. I felt dazed by all the changes, numb with loneliness for Yvonne. And I was afraid I'd wet the youth bed. In the middle of the night I got lost, feeling for the bathroom in the dark. Mrs. Scott ("Mother") found me in the dining room and led me gently to the toilet, and then back to bed. The next morning I awoke disoriented and apprehensive, trying to remember when, in the long night, I'd made my decision. I would not turn feisty and uncooperative, as I had at Miss Clara's. I would try to please, try to become worthy of this strange and lonely place.

"Becoming worthy" was something transplanted children practiced well. Adults seemed to believe, as long as some of the changes (especially material ones) were positive, that there should be little pain in the transition. Gratitude was the response expected from an adopted person.

Mrs. Scott insisted I be called by both names, Donna Ruth. Was this the name of a daughter who had died? Was I supposed to become her? What about Patty—was she so bad they finally just killed her?

And Jane. She had disappeared! To my anxious inquiry, Mother replied, "We won't discuss that now, sweetheart." She handed me instead the fragile doll (still unnamed) that she'd brought me after the Christmas play. I wanted big sturdy Jane, not this teeny sissy doll. I wanted to go home, to be Patty again.

But Patty was dead for sure. If I tried to bring her up, Mother would quickly change the subject. Yet she loved to talk about her own past, her family in Howard Lake, Minnesota. We would visit them "as soon as Lee has a day off work." Dad's name was Leonard, and various relatives and friends also called him Leo or Len.

"And Lee's late father, General Peter Scott," Mother told me proudly, "was the second mayor of Virginia, Minnesota. He named the town after his home state, where he'd had a large plantation. Later he became the American consul to French West Algiers." I felt no part of this family history; in fact, I felt like a complete fraud, using another girl's name and identity.

Questioning her, I learned they had not had a daughter. The name Ruth was for Mother's late sister, whom I resembled, and who had died at age nineteen of "infantile paralysis" (later called polio). Donna was simply a popular name at the time. She had considered naming me Rose Mary but was afraid I'd be called Rosie, which she hated.

They had given their son her maiden name, Patrick. In a final irony, Mother's nickname from nursing school, derived from her maiden name, was still used by Dad and his family. They called her Patty.

⌒ ⌒

I resumed second grade shortly after midyear in a white frame schoolhouse named for one of my book heroes, British nurse Edith Cavell. The school, standing just across the street from the Scotts' stucco bungalow, was my third school setting of this grim term that began at Miss Clara's. Somehow, in spite of the upheaval, I'd kept up with my schoolwork, so it was not academics that worried me. It was, of course, my differentness from the others, from children acquainted with each other, children long assimilated into their own families.

In those years, children who had been adopted at birth seldom shared that news with their grade school classmates. Frequently, in fact, adoptees did not learn of their backgrounds themselves until later, when they were "old enough to understand." Often, they were never told, or learned the truth by accident. The phenomenon was common enough that Hollywood produced several films about shocked teenagers discovering adoption papers while they were innocently looking for writing paper in their "parents'" desk. As a result, a whole generation of adolescents were suspicious and insecure about their origins. (If Mickey Rooney and Deanna Durbin didn't know the truth, they reasoned, then maybe I don't either.)

But there was no hiding my school-age adoption because our neighborhood on the northeast edge of the city was like a small town. With no competition yet from television, two- and four-party telephone lines buzzed with local news. For a while, I was a major topic—of curiosity mostly, and some derision. A few children avoided me, and occasionally I heard whispers.

"My mom says Donna Scott doesn't have any real parents," said one pinch-faced girl. Because of her, I have disliked pinch-faced people on first meeting ever since. (It is, of all my biases, the only one I recognized that I never tried to overcome.)

"No," said her confident friend, "she has to have a real mom someplace, but she doesn't got a real dad."

Other children would ask the dreaded questions: "Where's your real family?" "Did you have a mom who wasn't married?" It was much easier at the state school, where all of us were in the same boat. Here I knew of no other openly adopted child. Later, I would be amazed that every adoptee I met had lost both parents in a car crash (an explanation I sometimes resorted to myself), although none of my Owatonna friends had such clean-cut separations.

I could tell from their attitudes or questions which classmates came from homes where my arrival had been discussed with open acceptance. A few girls from those homes invited me to come and play after school. On the vines of those home visits, two special friendships ripened.

Luanne lived about half a mile away, not a long walk for seven-year-olds then. We spent a lot of time at her house, less at mine where our voices were hushed because Dad was night shift foreman for the Great Northern Railroad and slept during the day. Her parents were unpretentious and direct; I always knew where I stood with them. Luanne suffered from asthma, another condition that small playmates found hard to understand, and she had a brother close to Patrick's age, so we found an easy alliance despite her conventional beginnings. She was a caretaker child who finds the needy ones and shelters them with unquestioning friendship.

And she lived in a mansion! Actually, the family's comfortable living quarters were in one section of the large clubhouse her father, a professional golf teacher, managed for the city park board. With Luanne, I could roam its wonderful spaces—vast porches, a ballroom, soda fountain, and a storage room filled with rental golf clubs, toboggans, and skis. Luanne had been taught a careful respect for every foot of this public property, indoors and out, and I soon learned I could copy her example, or be sent home.

We had a mutual friend, and her name was Patricia. This Patty was our prettiest classmate, sensitive and delicate with older, somewhat protective parents. She wore her intense shyness well, softening it—with careful effort—into modesty and polite deference. Still, I believe her older sister, and the sister's friends, would have adopted demure Patricia as a powerless member of their own group if it hadn't been for Luanne and me. With us, her nervousness waned, her stutter almost disappeared.

Patty lived only a quarter mile away, but she had less free time to play and rarely came to my house. I felt good with both of my new friends. Even though we had arrived by different routes, we seemed to be in similar places now. We were good students, each with at least a small shadow to conquer, and we all had somehow developed rather generous spirits. Neither of them judged my "past," but I could mourn for Jane and one would offer to lend me her big doll as a substitute. I could say I was upset because Yvonne still hadn't written and then find notes in my desk:

"Can You come over after scool? LOVE, Luanne."

"What games do you think we shoud play at my birthday party? Plese anser in a letter. xxx ooo Patricia O."

There were some things I couldn't share, even with trusted new friends. The "honeymoon," my brief orientation into the family, was over, and Mother was determined to improve my neglected manners. She scolded me for responding to Patrick's "Wanna bet?" with "*You* wanna bet?" (Girls didn't say such things.)

I accepted the pinafores, bows, and curls that Mother preferred, just to keep peace. Habits and mannerisms could not be changed as easily. Besides, I never liked "niceness" for its own sake; I tried to be "good," but I had detected a difference early on. Stubbornly, emboldened by a few shreds of confidence gained from the approval of my friends and praise from my teacher, I clung to what was left of Patty Ann.

It wasn't long before I learned that the razor strop that hung alongside the bathroom sink could be more than a benign leather belt to hone Dad's straight razor. The argument would begin because I came home late from after-school play or "talked back" or was "loud and sassy." Eventually my tough jargon and manner would infuriate Mother. She would pull me to the garage (so we wouldn't wake Dad), and the thick hard strap would whack across the back of my thighs while I clung to the black Ford that had brought me to this state-sanctioned haven.

I was glad I could still fly a little, enough to transcend the sting from the welts, for now at least, and the sting from her angry words. I knew it added to her frustration that I wouldn't shed helpless tears.

Was this package of genetics and experiences I brought with me totally unacceptable to her? I felt she expected me to conform to the birth daughter of her fantasies. Like Proteus, the sea God who could change his shape at will. Like a bonsai tree, pruned to a new shape and form to fulfill one person's definition of delicate and lovely. But I was not an ornament. I had to grow somewhat as nature intended.

On some level I understood, even then, that there were flecks of gold to be panned from her advice. Even valuable nuggets, hard-gained from her own experience, that could enrich my life. But I did not yet feel secure enough here to abandon the toughness I had cultivated for survival, the independence that gave me some control. So I usually rejected her advice whole, out of stubborn defensiveness, and because her method was to criticize me instead of offering another choice for me to consider.

Yet, often, I glimpsed in my new mother the heart to nurture me well.

The first time I wet the new youth bed, I spread the covers up tight and hid my damp gown under my pillow. I learned then about Mother's sensitive nose. She walked into the bedroom, went straight to my bed, and pulled down the wool blanket and sheet. Sitting on Patrick's bed, I braced myself, but she came and sat beside me.

"If you have an accident, Donna Ruth," she said without a trace of anger or judgment, "you can put your sheets and nightgown in the laundry tub to soak, then please let me know." Gratefully, I watched her strip the bed. I saw there was a rubber sheet under the mattress pad. At least she was forewarned.

These times, when her tenderness warmed me, I vowed to try harder to behave, and to please her.

⌒ ⌒

At first I was wary of the stranger, Bud's age, whose bedroom I suddenly shared. But, although Patrick—whom I now called Pat—exercised an older sibling's prerogative to tease and boss me, I quickly learned that he could be trusted. And, fortunately for me, he wasn't a tattler. I believed Donna Ruth would be history too if Pat willed it. Mother believed in deferring to men in general, and indulging her only birth child in particular. I'm not certain why that bothered me so little. Maybe I thought it was a heavier burden for him than for me (he rarely exploited her favoritism). Or maybe I subconsciously accepted the premise that consciously offended me: that I should be grateful for things that birth children were allowed to take for granted, as though my background automatically endowed me with lower expectations.

And how did Pat feel, I wondered, about this spunky, sassy girl brought here to share his room—and his parents? Had he been offered any choice in the matter? Our unspoken feelings hung between my brother and me, separated by an almost tangible shroud of silence. I wondered what words his parents had used to convince this bright, sensitive boy to conform to their code of secrecy.

"Donna," Pat called to me one spring evening. (He was the only one Mother didn't correct if he occasionally used only my first name.) "How about a game of Monopoly?" He was confined to bed with one of his bouts of bronchitis.

Mother, a registered nurse, had worked at St. Mary's Hospital until her marriage. Any ailment that kept us from school would also restrict us under mounds of blankets while Mother monitored our temperatures, fluffed our pillows, and brought liquids at regular intervals. Whenever she assumed her professional role, she seemed confident and content, as if she were reliving happier times. And how

I wallowed in her long, expert back rubs! Her touch nourished both my body and my spirit.

It felt strange having a brother who was large and independent, the opposite of cuddly, drooling baby Duane. Pat didn't nurture me automatically as Yvonne had; I watched for the smallest protective gesture.

Our Monopoly game had become a marathon. Sprawled across the foot of Pat's bed, I watched him land next to my Park Place hotel.

"Oh, you're killing me," he said with a moan.

"Well, tough bounce!" I shot back. A voice from the open window reprimanded me. "Donna Ruth, I've told you not to use expressions like that!" Mother preferred to do her bend-and-twist exercises outside after dark as soon as the weather was mild enough.

I stuck out my tongue and shook a fist at the window. "What did you just do?" she asked angrily.

"Nothing," Pat said. "She's just shaking dice."

Once, though, even Pat couldn't influence Mother. She had discovered that Pat's beloved Duke had fleas. Although the dog stayed outside or in the back entrance, she panicked at the thought of tiny invaders leaping about the house and its occupants. She thought eradicating the fleas would be expensive and ineffective, so she gave Duke to the pound. (My alarm bells clanged; what would happen if I got head lice again?)

That night, hearing Pat's hard sobs in our dark room, my heart broke for him. While I shed my own silent tears, I expected to hear Duke on the back step. I couldn't believe Mother would go through with anything that hurt Pat so deeply. It was all the more surprising because I knew that Duke had been a replacement for Ranger, the German shepherd I'd seen on all of Pat's toddler pictures. That gentle dog had trailed a small Patrick through the fields behind our house until one day Ranger was accidentally hit by the car when Mother backed out of the garage with the same jerky motion she still created, letting the clutch fly out too quickly.

Pat had other dogs after Duke—a spitz, a terrier, and my favorite, a mongrel named Podunk. There was even a rude black Labrador retriever with a lineage more traceable than mine. But never another German shepherd, and none that my brother seemed to really love.

Becoming Donna

It was late spring, and the lilac hedge in our back yard had burst into blossom and scent before I made my first journey to Howard Lake to meet my new grandparents. Dad's monthly night off finally coincided with clear roads along the fifty-mile route.

More than a dozen people had assembled there for my extended-family debut, including their pastor and the pastor's son. It was confusing to meet so many at one time, and I would clearly remember only a few from that day.

Mother fussed with my hair and sash and coached my manners, obviously wanting me to make a good impression, but I didn't know what was expected of me. I studied the people who were comfortable here for clues, probing for common ground, but it was their unfamiliar, unique traits that popped out, demanded my attention. From this first visit, I would take away caricatures and an image of me, Alice in Wonderland, lost among Dickensian players from a very different drama.

Puckish Granddad Patrick, with his thatch of white hair, seemed

Dad's opposite, yet he listened, smiling and nodding, to Dad's views about events in Europe, labor unions, religion. Even schools, although Granddad had been a teacher, before accreditation was required. Now he was the custodian at the town's high school, loved by the students, staff, and parents, who all called him "Pat."

Grandmother Patrick was small, her back humped from labored breathing. Her graying brown hair was set into neat finger waves above a bun at the nape of her neck. Beneath a crisp apron, she wore a home-sewn silk dress, its white collar edged with her delicately crocheted lace. Although she suffered from severe asthma, a condition that forced the men to indulge their tobacco habits on the screened porch or in the basement, Grandmother tended a large garden. Three of her four bedrooms, all upstairs, were occupied by schoolteachers who paid room and board in exchange for her meticulous housekeeping and rich home cooking.

Aunt Mary, Mother's sister, was a genuine, salt-of-the-earth woman with tender eyes and a trust-inspiring manner. Her only adornments were the oversized tortoiseshell hairpins that held her pale-red hair in a figure eight twist on the back of her head. Her style of beauty required nothing more.

Mary's good-natured husband, Charlie Smith, had a rough reddish face below the line from his visor cap, but above his eyebrows his forehead was smooth and white, his balding head wrapped with the remaining strands of his red hair. He was the first farmer I'd ever met, and I was disappointed that, instead of the overalls I expected, he was wearing an ordinary shirt and tie.

Mother's handsome, exuberant brother Alvin had welcomed me best. As soon as we pulled into the driveway alongside my new grandparents' big old house, I scrambled from the car to breathe smokeless air, then stood waiting for Mother to gather her purse and sweater and the candy she'd brought. Pat, growing impatient, guided me ahead of him, hands on my shoulders, up the back steps and through the screened entrance into a large kitchen that smelled of bread and ham.

While the others clustered tentatively in the doorway to the dining room, Alvin turned from preparing food at the sink and wiped his hands on his apron. Knees bent and arms swinging, he performed an exaggerated strut across the kitchen.

"Well, here's that niece I've been hearing about. Lookee here!"— he affected an old-geezer voice—"We've added some real beauty to this old family!"

He squatted in front of me, generous pale blue eyes smiling beneath dark wavy hair, a huge grin on his face. "I hope you can cook," he said, now using his own pleasant baritone, squeezing my hand as he led me to the sink. "I've been waiting all day for a good helper." My eyes widened with wonder at this playful grown-up.

Uncle Alvin's tasteful jokes and knowing winks eased my tension many times that day, but I sensed that the adults tolerated his uninhibited style without really enjoying it. I learned many years later that he drank a bit. Maybe his family, all strict teetotalers, hesitated to indulge in pleasure, even secondhand, that might be enhanced by his "bad habit."

Alvin's wife, Aunt Nettie, was a delicate, quiet woman who spoke of her brother, a man called Freckles, in a serious tone that warned me, just in time, to turn away and hide my grin.

My four cousins included Mary and Charlie Smith's two boys and a girl—Vernon, Richard, and Mary—all older than Pat in two-year steps, and Nettie and Alvin's son, Billy, just two years older than I. Aunt Mary showed me a graduation portrait of her middle son, James, who had died of pneumonia the year before.

The word brought memories of Sally. Tears stung my eyes, hurt my throat. But then warmth and a smile as I thought how quickly she'd have become Alvin's co-conspirator, and she would not even have tried to suppress her giggle over the delightful absurdity of a grown man called Freckles!

None of my new relatives asked about my life prior to my metamorphosis from Patty to this new person they dutifully referred to as Donna Ruth. Only nine-year-old Billy (really Alvin William) decided to call me just Donna, and persisted until Mother finally quit correcting him. I liked him right away.

Before we went home, I learned another bit of family lore. In my grandmother's basement lived a man named Dean. He was her cousin (only a third cousin, Mother clarified), and no one else would take him in. They said he was "feeble-minded."

On my next trip to our grandparents' house, later in the summer, I got to know Billy better. Together we "stole" fat raspberries from Grandmother's garden and ate handfuls, warm and sweet, off the vine. While we licked our fingers clean, I studied this handsome cousin, this boy the same age as my sister, and noticed that his hair was just a shade lighter than Yvonne's. I wondered if, in winter, it darkened as hers did.

I was happy when Billy invited me to go fishing with him, his dad, and Granddad. All three were named Alvin, and they teased that they were surprised the women hadn't gotten together and named me Alvin too. I wasn't offended that they made light of my name change; their kind intent was clear. Sitting in the rowboat while Granddad baited my hook, I began to take root a little, tender shoots welcoming this nourishment so freely offered.

⌐ ⌐

In between those first two visits to Howard Lake, I experienced a day quite opposite from that calm day in the boat. With school recessed for the summer, Mother and I planned a day downtown.

I had discovered some ways to control my motion sickness on the streetcar. It helped to look only in the direction we were moving, not out side windows at objects whizzing by. Mother never hesitated to ask another passenger to move so I could sit in a front-facing seat, because sitting in a "peanut row" with my back to the side windows could also make me nauseated. If I felt sick anyway, Mother would get transfers from the motorman and help me to the curb, where I would take deep breaths to recover before the next car with our destination printed above the front window arrived.

But that warm June morning, with the streetcar's open windows admitting a fresh breeze, I managed the half-hour ride, jerky stops and all, with scant discomfort. Mother had an errand first at city hall. I was excited about the lunch and shopping that would follow.

I didn't recognize the courthouse when we climbed the stone steps, but once we were inside the cavernous lobby, I stared at the huge statue seated there and felt as if my blood had frozen in my veins.

"That is called 'Father of Waters,' Donna Ruth. It won't hurt you." Mother led me to the elevator. I trembled while we rode to the second floor and then walked down a long corridor. Mother found the office she wanted and sat me down on a bench inside the door. She sent me puzzled looks from her place in line until, her business done, she came to sit beside me.

"Do you feel all right?" she asked, her cool hand on my damp forehead. I stared at the deep pink flower that curved down the sloping brim of her straw hat. Her brown eyes were intent, questioning.

I couldn't tell her about the terror this place awakened in me: Daddy behind that screen, Momma with hands restraining her as she grabbed the air between us. Mother believed I was having a delayed reaction to the streetcar ride and decided to avoid the old building's lurching elevator. Beyond a door marked "exit," we found a stairwell. Our footsteps resounded on the steep stairs; my past became the reality while my present receded into the background along with the hollow echoes.

When we moved through the lobby I focused only on the passageway to our escape. On the sidewalk again, I thought I would pass out from holding my breath. While I clutched Mother's hand, we walked slowly a few blocks to the Woolworth store and took stools at the lunch counter. Mother ordered hot dogs for both of us, my favorite soda, and hot water for herself. While she took a tea bag from her purse and I sipped my 7UP, I half expected to see two women in sundresses and a row of children—a girl with reddish braids, and another with a short square bob.

But the mirror behind our waitress reflected a pale girl with light brown ringlets that touched her shoulders, wearing a blue hair ribbon that matched her dress. Beside her was an attractive woman with olive skin, a light touch of rose on her cheeks and lips, her dress a lighter shade of pink than the silk petals that decorated her hat.

Mother talked softly to our server, to me, to herself, I guess, while I mechanically ate this lunch I'd looked forward to for days.

"Donna Ruth, did you hear me?" she asked, dabbing at the corners of her mouth with a crumpled napkin. "If you're feeling better now, we'll go across the street to Dayton's." I was feeling better physically and thought I could recover my senses there as well as at home, so I nodded. The store's smooth elevator discharged us on a floor where women's dresses hung in colorful rows along the wall. Two children across the room caught my eye immediately—my cousins, Johnny and Jeanie! I hadn't seen them, except in pictures Momma brought on Owatonna visits, for nearly three years, but I was sure I was right.

A small blond woman accepted her package over the cash register, then turned and looked toward me. Aunt Ruth! I started to cross the open space, calling her name.

"Donna Ruth, stay here!" Mother called to me. By the time I reached the sales counter, my aunt had grabbed her children by the hands and turned to hurry away.

My face stung as if I'd been slapped. She saw me, knew me, but wouldn't acknowledge me! Why had she treated me that way? I only wanted to talk to her, ask about Momma. The secrecy I hated seemed to own my birth relatives too. Had they stopped speaking of me? Removed my pictures from their albums?

Mother was shaken too. Without a word, she led me in the opposite direction and out of the store, looking behind us as we walked to the corner. On the streetcar, she seemed calmer. "We're going home, sweetheart," she said, "and we'll eat that last big slice of watermelon." Amazing. She always insisted on leaving the last of any treat for the male members of our household.

From what Mother told me, I knew Leonard Scott had courted her relentlessly. They met as nurse and patient during the one hospital stay of his life, after he fell from a tall ladder while he was painting his mother's house. After his broken hip mended (leaving him with a pronounced limp), he took her to fancy restaurants, bought roses, and finally gave her an emerald-cut diamond, about three-fourths of a carat, set in platinum. Before their marriage, he bought their Tudor-style bungalow and furnished it with the Oriental rugs she wanted and a grandfather clock with Westminster chimes. For a wedding gift, she picked out a baby grand piano in rich mahogany wood.

She was twenty-seven, and he thirty-seven, when they married. She gave up her profession, a trade-off that was expected in a time when many employers, including airlines and the telephone company, dismissed women as soon as they married.

Dad became frugal the minute their vows were spoken. He had overspent to win the pretty, refined young nurse, but by nature he was more thrifty than even the stereotype of his Scottish heritage could possibly paint him. Dad's earlier marriage (which I would hear about accidentally ten years after joining the family) had taught him to keep tight control of his income.

Now he paid for everything with personal checks signed in his firm, authoritative hand. This included a monthly bill from the neighborhood grocer, whose delivery boy brought our order as often as Mother chose to call and place one. The weekly laundry was picked up and delivered too—not uncommon even for families of modest means when the alternative was a corrugated metal washboard for scrubbing, and clotheslines outdoors and in the basement. When the time came that Dad decided to buy a wringer washing machine, Mother stalled the purchase as long as possible.

The milkman delivered milk and cream every day, behind horses confident on their familiar route. He would set the milk inside the back entry and reclaim our bottles to be sterilized and reused. In winter, when the entryway's temperature dropped below freezing, the cream atop the milk (before homogenization ended the separation) would harden and push the paper cap off the bottle.

The iceman's insulated truck came three times a week to deliver a block of ice for the box in our back entry. The weight of the block was dictated by the number of pounds displayed on a large card in the customer's front window. We children would watch until the driver carried his load around to the back door on giant tongs, then boost ourselves into the open truck and grab a small piece of ice to suck on. He'd shake his fist as we ran away, pretending anger for the same reason we didn't just ask for the ice chips in the first place: it was more fun that way.

We dreaded the days Dad wrote checks for the household bills. He would remind us again to turn off lights as we left a room, and he would insist that Mother make better use of leftover food. Apparently those were the only lapses he could find in our adherence to his tight budget. Mother became adept at tricks, some touching, some imaginative, to pry money from Dad. Every year on her birthday, she received four crisp five-dollar bills in the mail. They came in five-cent greeting cards from my four aunts, two on Dad's side of the family, and Mother's sister Mary and sister-in-law Nettie. She would feign such surprise and excitement that Dad couldn't object to her plan to use the twenty dollars for crystal candleholders or a reproduction of a good painting or some other luxury she'd planned for months. Automatically, Dad provided the bills to reciprocate on the aunts' respective birthdays.

I asked Mother if it wasn't silly to send that money back and forth.

"Oh, no," she said, smiling. "Your aunts and I have that all worked out. It's a lovely way to get twenty dollars from our husbands."

From the beginning, I had to finagle everything the hard way, asking Dad for money for every purchase not covered by my meager allowance. Later, even trips to the drugstore for personal products had to be justified to him.

"Wait until he's had his breakfast," Mother would warn me. Or, "Don't try to talk to him until after supper." He rarely refused, but then I rarely asked for nonessentials, even forgoing the bike I wanted because the process was too demeaning, and I had to save my requests for school clothes. It was an unspoken rule that a girl needed a different outfit for every day of the week. Although I became a mix-and-match artist, I still operated barely on the side of respectability.

Once, I thought I'd get Pat's old fat-tired bicycle when he was saving for a new one. Then I learned that the old bike would be used as a trade-in. I settled for roller skates, and that time I avoided the postmeal economic summit meeting. I cut out a Sears Roebuck roller skate ad ("Clamps adjust to fit any shoe. Reg. price $2.19. Sale $1.99"), wrapped it with some cookies I'd baked, and tucked the bundle into Dad's lunch box with a note: "Roses are red, violets are blue. If I get the skates, I'll bake more for you." After school the next day, I found the ad and two dollars on my dresser, weighted down with my plaster figures of Snow White and Dopey.

I had shoplifted the two bright painted characters from the drugstore shelf while Mother was paying for a prescription. I found in them an irresistible reminder of my fourth birthday, a link to Daddy—and without hesitation I plucked them from a large display and shoved one into each coat pocket. Later, I told Mother I'd traded for them with Luanne, giving her a couple of Big Little books that Patrick gave me. It might confound some moralists (but hearten some parents) to know that, even though my dishonest deed went unpunished and totally unrepented, it was never repeated.

⌒ ⌒

Mother hated the surprise visits from the state agent who was monitoring my placement probation. The woman invariably dropped by when Mother's hair was set in metal curlers or the house was messy. Mother would signal me to be silent, and we'd hide until the frustrated caseworker left the front step. Eventually, she would have to call for an appointment, and then Mother would be a nervous wreck preparing for her visit.

Mother's concern about the child welfare people's reaction surprised me because, when I made her especially angry, she would tell me, "We don't have to keep you here if you can't mind" and "If you don't like the rules here, you can always go back where you came from." I'm sure she believed her threats would frighten me into obedience, not fathoming what deep resentment and hurt they fostered.

Still, Mother was a woman of moods and mystery, nourishing me in short bursts, when she could. Patting some Pond's cold cream on her face, she'd smile at me in the mirror.

"I wish I'd had you sooner," she would say. I examined her words. Did she mean she could have produced a better me? But no, there was no disapproval in her voice; she said it wistfully, as if she had missed something special. Her words were salve to my damaged parts, but only a more sustained flow of love could bring trust and stability to this life so filled with absence.

My adoption agreement had relied on the Scotts' promise to finish a room upstairs for Pat, giving me the back bedroom. They had only to add dormer windows, heat ducts, and some insulation to convert the attic, but they kept putting off the expense. Actually, they seemed to be in no hurry to complete the adoption, and I wondered why they had bothered. One day I found the courage to ask Mother why they had wanted me. Her answer wasn't reassuring.

"I wanted to adopt the little twin boys we saw there," she said. Her answer rang true because often, when I asked why Pat could do something and I couldn't, she would respond, "Because he's a boy." (Never "Because he's older than you are.") It appeared that my gender, as well as my genetics, disappointed her. Well, I could do nothing about either one.

"But," she continued, "Lee thought we should get an older girl who could help me around the house." His desire for a clean house was understandable; her housekeeping fell far short of her mother's. But until that conversation, I'd taken pride in my growing list of household chores, believing they came with membership in the family. Now it seemed they were one more condition of my being accepted.

Mother seemed oblivious to the demoralizing impact of her words, but to me these revelations were startling. I was sorry that I had asked.

⌒ ⌒

Mother's effusive social manner charmed most people who met her. In the women's auxiliary to Dad's Masonic Lodge, she was popular with everyone, but sought out several women who were married to professional men. Comparing her own clothes, house, and social life to theirs seemed to increase her dissatisfaction.

But her best friend from that group, Ceile, benefited greatly from Mother's friendship. Ceile, a dentist's wife, had a heart condition so serious that her husband had a chair lift installed on their stairway. Mother's easy acceptance of her friend's limitations, her focus on Ceile's strengths, helped the fragile woman feel calm and confident when she was well enough to venture out. And all the while, behind the scenes, Mother effectively used her entire allotment of righteous indignation to squelch the inevitable rumors that questioned the handsome dentist's faithfulness to his sick wife.

Ceile was still young when she suffered a fatal heart attack. I arrived home from school to find Mother, alone in the kitchen, moaning softly, "Ceile, oh my darling Ceile." I put my arms around her as she slumped on a stool by the sink. She sobbed on my shoulder, and I could physically feel her pain at the loss of her friend. Patting her back, I cried too, finally, for Sally—and for all the other loved ones I had lost. And once again, the unwritten rule that silenced my words was the heaviest burden of all.

Several Italian-American families lived on our block; some shared the same extended family. They were working-class families too, all with one male wage earner, and they were impressed with Mother's nursing degree. Often, when one of their children was sick, they'd call Mrs. Scott for advice before spending a few precious dollars to consult their doctor.

"I'm so sorry she's ill, Rose," I'd hear her say on the phone. "You keep her warm, and I'll be right over." She'd take her thermometer from the mirrored bathroom cabinet and hurry over to evaluate the child's symptoms. Occasionally, suspecting a serious or communicable disease, she'd advise them what to tell the doctor. More often, she'd suggest bed rest, aspirin for a fever, and lots of liquids. Always, she'd monitor the progress of her patients by phone or visits until they were back to normal.

Our neighbors repaid her with gifts of food. The man next door, a driver for Ives Ice Cream Company, would bring a carton of Popsicles or Fudgsicles packed in dry ice. Another neighbor brought her homemade pizza—a dish barely known in this country then. Mother's sensitive nose was overwhelmed by the strong, unfamiliar cheese and spices, and she refused to bring it into the kitchen. She'd let the pizza cool on top of the icebox in the back entrance, then wrap it in layers of newspaper—and still worry that dogs might detect it in the garbage and scatter it where the thoughtful giver might see it. Of course, she would tell our neighbor that the pizza was incredibly good. "So *won*-der-ful," in fact, "it should definitely be on the market."

I was frustrated that she wouldn't let me try this tempting new food. She knew the kitchen it came from was fastidiously clean, the ingredients quite healthful. Within a few years, that neighbor took Mother's insistent advice to heart and began selling her pizza to small grocery stores, then supermarkets, spawning a business that eventually sold for $20 million. When I buy that brand now, I still mourn the waste of those individually created samples.

꼭   ꒻

With relief, I welcomed fall's emerging colors. I wasn't sure it happened in this place.

My favorite season felt different here; no groups of orphans jumping into leaves, then tramping inside with drippy noses to remove their dusty jackets and slurp bowls of steamy soup. Nor was it like the first fall I remembered, when that blistering-hot summer gave way to blustery days with scant evidence of autumn in between—just bare wooden poles rising from the concrete that surrounded our apartment.

This fall of 1940 was a glorious one; Indian summer days lingered past the start of November. I began the Armistice Day holiday playing outside wearing a light sweater. The rain that forced me inside soon turned to sleet. At lunchtime, I dragged my snowsuit from the back of the closet, searched for mittens, and carried black buckle over-shoes up from the basement. They were too small to fit over my new saddle shoes, so I put them on over double socks.

Outside again, I made angels in the fresh snow. Then Patrick joined me, and we built a fort from hard-packed balls of the rapidly falling wet flakes. Finally, unable to see beyond the reach of an arm through the frenzied wind-spun snow, we heeded Mother's third call to come inside.

That night, even Dad's tire chains couldn't guarantee his prompt midnight arrival at work. Although he started out (against radio warnings) two hours early, he had to abandon his car halfway to the round-house. Fortunately, a truck driver rescued him as he was plodding along the deserted street in his sheepskin coat and steel-toed safety shoes. But 144 people, from the southwestern states to New England, died of exposure in the Great Armistice Day Blizzard. There were fifty-nine deaths in Minnesota, where the twenty-four-hour snowfall varied from sixteen to twenty-six inches, catching hunters and commuters by surprise.

Dad stayed at the roundhouse for a couple of days, until minimal movement was restored. The three of us were snowed in and, spoiled by frequent grocery deliveries, running short of food. Deep snow was packed so hard against the outside doors that we couldn't open them until Patrick climbed out through a window and shoveled the four-foot drifts away.

After that, the wooden shelves in the basement held at least a week's supply of food—canned salmon, soups, as much variety as possible within the limited choices of the grocer's stock and Mother's preference for plain, nonethnic food.

The country roads were cleared in time for our Thanksgiving trip to my grandparents' Howard Lake home. Its warmth enfolded us after our long slippery ride, with Patrick watching me closely for signs that I might upchuck and spray him as I had once before.

The whole family was there, plus one of Grandmother's boarders who couldn't get home, and a couple of people who, she'd heard through the church or school, would otherwise be alone on the holiday.

Uncle Alvin deftly removed sage-y stuffing from a golden-brown turkey, then set it on a table that groaned under its Norman Rockwell display of food. The traditional array was crowned with Aunt Mary's incomparable pies—pumpkin, mincemeat, and, just for me, the peach one she knew I loved.

With my head bowed, I listened to Granddad's simple, sincere prayer of thanks and wanted to share his gratitude for this food and family. But don't they belong to Donna Ruth? I wondered. Would Patty be welcome here? The answer that came to me was not logical, except to a confused child one month from her eighth birthday. In my heart, I felt sure Aunt Mary would have made the pie for Patty, if she had known her.

I watched Granddad lift generous slices on his carving knife and pass the first plates down the table to the two people I'd never met until today. Some kind of relief, maybe at not having to prove myself here, surged through me until it tingled in small feet that dangled well above the floor. I wore, on that holiday, new patent leather shoes. Mother had shown me how to rub them with olive oil "so they won't crack," being careful not to stain the grosgrain bow. To this day, the scent of olive oil reminds me of shiny black shoes.

chapter eight

A New Family Tree

Give me a child until he is seven,
and I will show you the man.

JESUIT SAYING

I was not yet familiar with this saying, so I didn't suspect I should
be fully formed. I kept trying to reinvent myself, to become a
creature with a clean past and a secure future.

I gathered up the strands of my life—stifled secrets, dark dreams,
fading memories—and tried to force them into a new fabric. But
they did not lie flat and neat, woven through like the yarn that grew
into soft afghans beneath Grandmother's rhythmic needles. There
were frayed and knotted places. The damaged ends, receiving no attention, seemed unlikely to mend by themselves.

Dad ruled the household with a steady hand and iron will, pro-
moting responsibility above all. Where I had always longed for more
diversity, more discovery, he valued conformity and repetition.

Every Christmas, and often in between, Dad told of a long-ago holiday accident, when the sash from his little sister's dress caught fire from a candle on their tree. Though Dad was just a young lad, he quickly clapped out the flames with his bare hands and rescued small Dorothy from injury. While his mother treated his burns, his father merely laid a hand on his shoulder and said "Good boy." Dad's face would grow serious, his eyes misty, when he repeated the two words. It was obviously a milestone in his quest for his father's approval. Now Dad stopped at the home of his feisty widowed mother one morning every week on his way home from work. Gram was a perfectly proportioned miniature lady, more than ninety years old, who weighed barely a pound per year. When Dad stepped into her plain tidy kitchen, he might find her scrubbing the floor on her hands and knees. Her daughter Dorothy, a single woman of forty-three, would be leaving for her job as a supervisor for the telephone company.

"Don't work too hard, Mother," she would say.

"Hard work," Gram would snap, "never hurt a living soul."

Aunt Dorothy would laugh. "Would you explain to her, Leo, that it's her heart I'm worried about?"

Dad had gone to his younger sister's rescue another time, nursing her back to health during the devastating influenza pandemic of 1918. The illness did leave Dode, as Dad called her, with her hair turned cotton-white. It also took the life of their brother William.

Dad's father, in the end, had chosen to lavish his favor and fortune on four offspring by his first wife, a talented and beautiful woman who had died young. He left a small pension for Gram and nothing for Aunt Dorothy and Dad, the daughter and surviving son of his second marriage.

On Gram's infrequent visits to our house, she would reach into her little black drawstring coin purse with a hand heavy-veined, like the underside of a leaf, and draw out one quarter each for Pat and me. I'd kiss her feather-soft cheek and relish the feel of her arms wrapped around me.

Dad spoke of his mother and sister in a tone of concern that seemed reserved just for them. Mother noticed it too, and reacted as if they were her rivals.

"Dode says hello," he'd report, arriving home from his weekly visit, "and Ma sent this homemade apple pie."

"Not for me," Mother would say. "She knows I can't eat pies made with lard instead of butter!"

Dad would fall uncharacteristically silent, avoiding this tired battle.

Occasionally, on friendlier mornings, he would approach Mother's back while she stood at the stove making breakfast. His arms would circle her waist, and he would nuzzle her neck. Later, I'd hear them whispering, moving in their bed behind the closed door.

I knew Dad was proud of Patrick. It was obvious in the way he gave Patrick his full attention, in the way he looked at his son when he walked away. But I don't know if he ever told my brother how special he was, and I'm sure he never said "I love you."

Dad was slightly more demonstrative with me, although, like him, I concealed my needy side well. He would take me on his lap while he taught me to tell time on his pocket watch, its gold worn thin on top, next to the stem where he wound it.

When I was approaching my ninth birthday I got a clear message, through Mother's unambiguous nonverbal language, that she thought I was too old to sit on Dad's lap.

So on an afternoon in early December I lay next to his chair, working the crossword puzzle in the *Minneapolis Sunday Tribune and Star Journal*. Dad rose earlier, on Sunday afternoons, to have dinner with Mother, Pat, and me—all hungry after returning from Sunday school and morning service at Wesleyan Methodist Church. Often the minister, encouraged by shouts from the male worshipers ("Amen, Brother!" "Yes! Praise the Lord!"), would go on for an extra half hour.

While Mother readied this Sunday meal (it would have been roast beef, baked ham, or fried chicken), Dad read the paper and switched on the radio.

The announcer's voice sounded urgent: ". . . six battleships were sunk and 164 airplanes destroyed before they could leave the ground." (The statistics would, in later bulletins, include damaged equipment.)

We learned that every Saturday night the battleships of the diminished American fleet in the Pacific tied up in pairs at their moorings while crews were given liberty in Honolulu. That morning, carrier-based Japanese planes came in from the north, around the cloudy mountains, and bombed the fleet to bits.

The next day, the aristocratic voice of President Franklin Delano Roosevelt echoed through the hallway of our grade school, calling the previous day "a date which will live in infamy." The president was now in his third term and would be elected to a fourth before he died. This man, so strong in his wheelchair, was already the most familiar, most continuous male presence in my life.

Even before the nearly twenty-five hundred bodies from the Pearl Harbor slaughter were buried, there was talk of rationing and government takeover of plants that now made Coca-Cola, Kodak cameras, and Quaker Oats. No one doubted that the country was in crisis.

By the following Sunday, war had been declared and troops were in motion. Dad was still up, absorbed in newscasts and newspaper, when we returned from church, where the pastor had not departed from his theme of salvation versus damnation.

⌒ ⌒

My adoption was finalized without fanfare (to preserve our myth of normal relationship) nearly two and a half years after my arrival. I was tired of pretending it was normal to be uprooted from one's childhood home, wrenched from a birth family. I needed someone to acknowledge that I was part of a wounded minority, that small percentage of the population who walk around looking like everyone else, concealing hidden scars.

And I wondered, if adoption was so "normal," why radio and newspaper reports always referred to a celebrity's "adopted" son or daughter by that nonbirthright status, even when the adoptee was full grown.

The state, in granting my adoption petition, accepted the installation of dormer windows as proof that the attic conversion would soon be completed. In fact, it would be nearly three more years.

One day Mother chastised me for entering "Pat's bedroom" wearing only an undershirt and panties.

"It's my bedroom too," I said.

The next day, a roll-away bed was unfolded in the dining room, squeezed between the mahogany dining table and the double windows hung with rose brocade draperies. I would sleep there, although my clothes remained in their assigned space in Pat's bedroom.

Now it was impossible to sleep until after Dad left for work at 11:30. His voice, though calm and low, could be heard plainly through the swinging door to the kitchen, where he sat overdosing on strong coffee for the long night ahead.

In winter, I'd bring Dad's heavy sheepskin coat from the front hall closet and, on tiptoe, try to boost it over his shoulders while he balanced his weight with a cane. The hip he'd broken sixteen years earlier was growing steadily worse, but he refused the socket replacement surgery he needed because its failure rate was still high. At age fifty-two, he was already so obviously in pain that I hated to see him step from the warm kitchen into the bitter night. I would hear the rattle of the garage door as he slid it open and the squeak of tires on the snow—or the clank of chains the tires wore when the snow was deep. I knew he was mentally planting his sunny abundant garden.

☙ ❧

Beyond our garage the grassy fields, silent now under the snow, would spring to life untended, providing habitat for dozens of plant and animal species.

Our neighbors' homes huddled close along our block to the south, but to the north a wooded area remained. I climbed its trees and preserved their autumn leaves. I ironed them between waxed paper, carefully, with the waxed sides of the paper next to the leaf, then taped the transparencies in windows to prolong the color that had flared too briefly in my early black and white years.

The owner of the three wooded lots charged Dad just ten dollars a year for the use of a wide strip of land between our house and the woods. The man even tilled the plot each spring; patriotic "victory gardens" were encouraged. Dad repaid him with vegetables when the harvest peaked.

The summer I was ten, red surveyor's stakes warned of the destruction of the habitat, the woods, and even Dad's garden. Dad pur-

chased, for back taxes, eight lots (four acres) in a sparsely developed
area just outside the city limits, about two miles north of us. He
planned to recoup the annual taxes on the property by managing
about half of it as a truck farm, growing vegetables to last the winter.
He gained Mother's promise to preserve all this produce by agreeing
to build a new house on one of the lots when the area developed so
he could sell the other seven at a good profit.

Mother chose her lot on a knoll overlooking a tiny lake shaped
roughly like a heart. She planted a dozen birch trees around the
boundaries of the property and down the gentle slope to Hart Lake
and named the modest domain Birch Acres.

Mother's self-imposed chore then was to haul water for her birch
trees. Dad tied a huge barrel, discarded at the roundhouse, to the
back of an old Graham-Paige car he'd bought in order to qualify for
additional gas rationing stamps. He had a "C" sticker (maximum gas
allowance) for the car he used for his railroad job, which the government deemed essential. The Graham-Paige, as a second vehicle, had
been granted an "A" sticker, good for only three gallons a week.
Now, as a conveyor of food grown to supplement a family's income,
it was upgraded to "B" status. The government's regulations were
outnumbered only by exceptions to the rules.

The responses to food and gas rationing, even amid gung ho support for the war, were often creative. In addition to the predictable
black markets in nylons, coffee, and sugar, youthful innovators
burned stove gas in the family car to disguise their actual mileage. (It
pinged a little when the driver accelerated, but it made the car
move.)

My mother received the extra sugar stamps she needed for her
berry jams and canned fruits as payment from her unofficial patients.
Apparently our Italian neighbors used less sugar in their herb-rich
cooking.

I had enjoyed helping Dad tend his small garden, feeling a certain
camaraderie as his productive partner. (Patrick, by now, had liberated
himself from planting and weeding by finding teen employment at
golf courses, cemeteries, anywhere paid work was available.)

But now, every weekday morning all summer, I was up and
dressed before Dad arrived home from work at 8:30. He and I would

eat a quick breakfast, and arrive at "the garden," as he called it, about 9:00.

I knew Dad enjoyed this total change from his night job. Working in sunlight seemed to invigorate him, even though the work was physically hard for him. He sat on a low stool to pick raspberries and dig potatoes. He needed both hands on his cane to pull himself to his standing position, now bent slightly forward, one hip protruding unevenly.

For me, the tiring hours of work in the big garden held scant redeeming value, only heat and dust, the pesky gnats and disconcerting bees. But I had no more choice than the young field hands at Owatonna.

⌐ ⌐

In the driveway of Birch Acres—really two ruts divided by a strip of weeds—at noon each summer weekday (unless my prayer for rain had been answered), Dad climbed stiffly into the rusty Graham-Paige and called to me, "C'mon, Snooks, didn't you hear that lunch whistle blowin'?" The nickname was borrowed from Fanny Brice's radio child, "Baby Snooks." It was Dad's way around my cumbersome, maternally mandated alias.

We would drive home to devour the hearty lunch Mother had prepared. Dad talked to Mother between bites, sitting there with his forehead red-rimmed from the sweatband on his straw Panama "garden" hat. I was excused now from dishes and other chores until Saturday, but I would set to work on the back step shelling a dishpan full of peas or picking over pails of beans. Dad retired to his room for the rest of the day. Mother had aired it all morning so she could close the windows now against the outdoor sounds and shroud them in black flannel to shut out the day. By the time I washed the garden grime from my sunburned body and gave up trying to clean my fingernails, the afternoon was spent. My school friends had slept later and shaken some rugs or washed breakfast dishes before pairing off for a day of outdoor play. I knew that, at three in the afternoon, it would be useless to phone around. Usually, I could find one of my two "summer friends" outside if I walked over to their yards in the next block.

Kay was two years older than I, a big solid girl. Together we

looked like a four-year age difference. Mother disapproved of her because she "talked about older things"—like the physical attributes of
boys who dated her slim and sophisticated older sister, Linda.

Kay was too clumsy to join me on the horizontal bars in the school
yard or to roller-skate up and down our sloping narrow sidewalk, but
she was obsessed with the Roller Derby and went there often with
her grandmother. Kay described the brutal bumps and shoves of the
races with relish. Her descriptions were vivid enough; I quickly declined her invitation to see one myself.

We would sit in Kay's back yard eating, she because she was hungry and I because the food was there.

"My sister cut the pointy ends off her bra cups," Kay whispered.

"Why?" I asked, fascinated.

"Linda saw a picture, in Grandma's old movie magazine, of Jean
Harlow wearing a cream satin bias-cut slip dress and no brassiere. She
says having her bare nipples rub on a silk blouse all day drives her
crazy." As usual, she told me a little more than I cared to know, but
at least it accounted for sixteen-year-old Linda's sultry pout.

Frail Shirley, nearly two years my junior, lived directly across the
street from Kay, but they never talked to each other, even in that
child-scarce neighborhood. Besides their four-year age gap, Kay's
haughty mother disapproved of Shirley's single mom.

Shirley had to stay close to home, to help the old woman who
cared for her and her two siblings while their mom worked. My
mother didn't like Shirley's mom either, although they had never
met.

"I'd never go to work and leave my children to be raised by a
stranger," Mother said, ignoring the absence of an alternate breadwinner for the young family. "If the communists take over our country, they'll put all the mothers to work and force all the children into
state-run day care," she said, reciting one of the more chilling popular predictions of the day.

Besides, she'd seen blond, shapely Sheila (who let me call her by
her first name) in her shorts and halter, bending to weed her flower
garden one day as Mother drove by with Patrick beside her.

Of course, I adored Sheila, who looked like an actress and went
barefoot around the house just like her kids, singing all the popular

lyrics along with her radio, in between dainty puffs on a cigarette. Shirley and I would try on Sheila's hats and high heels, and use her nail polish. We rated all her boyfriends on a point system that evaluated their looks, the cars they drove, and their friendliness toward us. Some of them unknowingly upped their scores by giving us gum or small change. No one told us we shouldn't accept their gifts. Fortunately for us, their dubious intentions were all directed at Shirley's mother.

My sixth grade classroom smelled of chalk dust and ink and the lavender water Miss Kroger wore. Wells of ink were recessed into every desk. Our thirsty fountain pens slurped in ink with a flick of the feed lever, then we wiped the points with small cloths. There was something about this ritual of preparing to write that lent importance to the activity.

The room also smelled of apples, peanut butter, Fig Newtons— any scent strong enough to escape the brown paper bags squashed under some of the desktops. It was a blessing that I, with my touchy stomach, lived close enough to go home for lunch. Home to a kitchen that smelled of vegetable soup or a grilled Velveeta cheese sandwich or (my favorite) hot milk and garden peas poured over buttered toast. If Mother was in a good mood, she'd talk to me while I ate. Sometimes I'd find her lying on Pat's bed, facing the wall, and I'd tiptoe out, taking my library book for company.

I liked to sit in class and draw; it helped me see elusive things more clearly. One day Miss Kroger (rhymes with *ogre*) was busy opening windows from the top, using a long pole with a hook on the end. When she reached up, her ample bosom rose to reveal her belt. Her eyeglasses, hanging from a chain, rose and fell with each deep breath.

I began drawing Kay's sister's boobs, poking through the clipped, frayed brassiere. I wanted to see what they looked like, standing hard under the silk shirt. My curiosity satisfied, I was folding the paper when I saw Miss Kroger's large hand reaching out. I respectfully declined, but she took it anyway, and unfolded it, and *looked* at it, while my face turned hot and crimson. She frowned disgustedly; I winced sheepishly. When she crumpled the paper, my relief was immense. The incident reigned for quite a while as my most humiliating moment, until it was replaced with another—too horrible to mention.

Dwelling on the traumatic event later, I decided Mother must be right about my inbred crudeness; a discouraging thought. At the same time, it struck me that my traumas these days, while still painful in their way, were on a smaller scale than many of Patty's had been. Still, I shared the Linda-boob story with no one on earth. There were, I decided, some things that truly were shameful enough to deserve secrecy.

⌒ ⌒

I never lied to my father. In spite of all his faults, I believed in his honesty. I also believed his piercing blue eyes could see into my mind. Working at the garden, mid-morning one torrid day, I felt weak and faint. A budding twelve-year-old, sweating in shorts and a tank top, I was doubled over with menstrual cramps. I asked Dad to take me home. He decided, against all the evidence of my uncomplaining work over several summers, that I was goldbricking.

"If you're too sick to work," he said, grinning, "you better go home."

I felt abandoned again. My anger kept me going for the first mile, until I had to sit awhile on a curb, afraid I'd pass out from pain and stifling heat. I wished I'd brought my thermos of water from the car. Eventually I trekked the remaining mile, focusing on home, aspirin, a drink of ice water, and a hot water bottle against my stomach.

I was only half a block from home when Dad drove by me. He beeped the horn and waved, grinning again as he passed. I ran the remaining distance with my heart trying to pop out of my chest and then burst through our back door before he could limp up the walk. I screamed to Mother, "He's a mean shitty bastard. I don't want to talk to him—ever!" She was too surprised to react to my street language.

I slammed two doors on my way to the bathroom to change a soaked pad and cry my eyes out. When I emerged, Mother was still scolding him: "You always think you know everything! She's not a horse, you know!'' He looked sheepish over his lunch when I made a necessary trip to the kitchen for pain relievers, but he didn't apologize. It would have surprised me greatly if he had.

Mother did believe in apologies, and I vividly remember one she gave me. We were getting along better, in these weeks since I'd graduated from grade school, but an argument began over my wearing makeup. She, who wore little of it herself, flatly refused. Standing over the sink washing dishes, I turned to her. She was seated on the stool, dish towel in hand.

''You don't know what you're talking about,'' I said tersely. ''You sit in this house and you don't know what's going on.''

I'd hit a raw nerve. She grabbed my arm and said stiffly, ''If you think it's so terrible here, you can still go back where you came from.'' She resurrected the dread words I'd buried deep inside, down where all the pain and confusion and rejection hid. Words that hadn't been spoken since my adoption became final. I crumbled under the weight of them, this time unable to hold back the torrent of tears. I wept bitterly, slumped over the sink, her arms holding me while she repeated helplessly, ''I'm sorry. Oh! I'm so sorry.''

⇌

I'd complained of poor vision all during sixth grade, where I sat at a front desk in order to read the blackboard. The school nurse decided I must be faking when I couldn't read the eye chart's third line. No one, she was sure, could do so well in school and be that blind. Mother accepted the nurse's opinion because she already suspected I wanted glasses; she'd seen me try on a friend's new pair with interest and curiosity.

Finally, noticing that I held books eight inches from my eyes, she decided to take me to her eye doctor. He confirmed a total deficit below the chart's top two lines. When we returned for my glasses, I was astonished to see clearly, from the doctor's twelfth-floor window, cars and people moving below.

At home, walking with Mother from the garage, I said, ''The blades of grass look separate now.'' I could see, too, her eyes glistening as she looked down at me gently. This time her apology was unspoken, silenced by the lump in her throat. I could see she was suffering from not trusting me. Maybe, just maybe, I should try to trust her motives more too.

☞ ☜

My new glasses and I started junior high in the fall of 1944. I had prepared carefully, wisely trimming off my long spiral curls early in the summer, then exchanging Toni home permanents with Patricia. We had beginner's luck (or amazing skill, if you asked us). Hers produced the springy short curls she desired in place of her soft waves; mine added body and loose waves to my baby-fine hair. By fall the waves were gone, but my medium-length pageboy haircut retained some of the bounce promoted by the Toni twins in *Seventeen* magazine. I held the magazine ad next to my face in the mirror. Except for my glasses, I decided, we could be triplets.

Mother didn't agree. "First your pretty curls," she said mournfully, "and now those glasses." Nor did she like the long straight skirts (one tan, one glen plaid) that I'd chosen for school. Or the tailored shirts, a yellow one and a blue one, to wear under my neutral cardigan or alone.

But I knew I could concoct several outfits, adding scarves or jewelry I'd borrow from Mother's drawers or the attic. Luanne was going to help me make a jumper; it would be of burgundy corduroy. I was tingly-excited as I slipped shiny pennies into the slots of my pleasant-smelling new loafers.

The brick school building nine blocks from our house seemed large and challenging. Children from two other grade schools merged there. We would have different teachers for each subject now, and a couple of them were men! It felt like a fresh start for me, more equal now with the other kids. The whispers about my adoption had all but ended. New friends would know only what I chose to tell them.

The boys I knew had changed radically over this summer. Where had their cracking voices gone? Now their wisecracks were delivered in short deep bursts. Their careful boy-walks had become slack, almost disjointed. Shoulders swung loosely too, in leather-sleeved wool jackets. Their legs in the mysterious jeans were never quite still. Standing, they shifted their weight from one leg to the other, and when they sat, their feet moved restlessly under their desks. And oh, what cute narrow butts beneath those widening shoulders!

Funny, I hadn't noticed it in such detail when my brother passed this stage four years ago. Now he was a popular junior at the bigger, still more distant high school. He worked ably in the meat department of our grocery store, then rushed home to shower and change for a date or an evening with friends. He seemed to have outgrown the house. I was afraid he would outgrow us all.

Once, Pat handed me his theme paper, asking if I'd check the grammar and punctuation. His assignment was to recollect the worst and best events of his life. I don't recall his "worst" example, but his choice of "best" startled me.

"The best," he wrote, "was when we adopted my sister, because there was more talking and fun and laughing in the house."

So this house had felt quiet and lonely to him too. And my coming had cheered him! I was glad he'd found a way to let me know.

Mother discussed romance and men with me, but never sex. She taught me the proper medical terms for body parts and functions, but neglected to warn me about menstruation. (I thought I was dying.)

My seventh grade science teacher was young, pretty, and interesting—a combination much more rare in teachers then than it is now. Unlike all my grade school teachers, she was married.

Mrs. Kirchner took it upon herself to introduce sex education into our biology unit. She would leave the curious boys in the classroom, with a monitor in charge, and herd the girls into a small lab with a screen and projector. She would show a brief contraband film, then coax from us a few stammered questions that exposed the depth of our ignorance. After about twenty minutes, we returned red-faced to the classroom and the boys followed Mrs. Kirchner out the door, trying to look nonchalant. We had barely finished her section on menstruation, too late for me and half the other girls (and I suppose the boys' news about nocturnal emissions was tardy too), when Mrs. Kirchner was fired. As upset as most of the students were, we were unable to convince our parents to protest her dismissal.

For many of us, any future discussions of our bodies or reproduction would be full of giggles, mystery, and gross inaccuracies.

Winds of Change

Seventh grade, with all my new feelings and freedoms, turned suddenly grim, first interrupted by Grandmother Patrick's frequent illnesses. I remembered occasional sudden train trips to Howard Lake during my last two years of elementary school. Mother and I rode the night train, using Dad's railroad pass; I jerked sleepily from side to side, leaning against Mother's shoulder, trying not to be sick. The conductor would call out a town's name as we approached the depot that stood in soft-lit welcome between the tracks and the silent town. "*Way*zata," he called, announcing our first stop. "*Long* Lake." He accented each on the first syllable, in a voice geared to wake dozing travelers. "*Ma*ple Plain, *De*lano, *Mon*trose, *Wa*verly, *How*ard Lake." If a station required no stop that night, the passing train whipped the mailbag off its hook as it sped by, while quick hands flung the incoming mail onto the station platform.

Arriving in Howard Lake after midnight, we carried our suitcases the three blocks to my grandparents' house. Granddad had left a light burning on the screened porch. We slipped quietly into the kitchen, unhampered by unnecessary locks. Mother's expert nursing had Grandmother on her feet in a few days.

This winter, Grandmother's asthma confined her to bed often. Mother went to her alone; I stayed home to take care of my schoolwork and the family housework.

Then it was time for my lovely spring vacation (too early to plant Dad's garden but warm enough for long walks with friends. Yes, God, I'm alive!). But Dad decided I was capable enough, at age twelve, to care for my grandmother and her boarders for a week, to give Mother a needed break.

It was nothing like the annual pleasant week of summer I'd enjoyed there when Grandmother was well, attending Bible school, the city girl making small-town friends. My grandmother, on those occasions, had been gentle to me, generous with her time and instruction. A proper English lady, she pronounced her daughters' names "Maeri" and "Law-rah" and always referred to her son (named also for her father, Austin Merriman) as Alvin Austin. This gentility, combined with her frontierlike strengths, left me in awe of her. Her smile was centered in her eyes and high cheekbones. (Mother's widemouthed laugh that involved her whole face, that wrinkled her nose and squinted her eyes, was a gift from her bonny Irish father—a gift she passed on to Patrick.)

On this compulsory visit, I ran the stairs constantly to deliver Grandmother's juice, water, meals, and medicine. In between, Granddad good-naturedly taught me the exact way to prepare supper for the boarders. I knew he'd just as soon give them an apology and a sandwich, but he thought our effort was a cheap price to pay for keeping Grandmother calm.

But calm she was not. Granddad would urge me to take a break, and I'd pick up one of their religious publications (well, there were a few jokes and a crossword puzzle in them), or their *Saturday Evening Post*, and then Grandmother would ring her loud bell.

"Donna Ruth, did you put those clean sheets on all the ladies' beds?"

I didn't tell either one of them about Dean, Grandmother's basement-recluse cousin. He had coaxed me further into his room when I brought his tray downstairs, saying he had something to show me.

Suddenly he grabbed me, brushed his bony hands down the front of my body and tried to put his grinning toothless mouth against my face. I pushed him away, ran trembling up the stairs to the empty kitchen, and cried with my face in my hands while the boarders' potatoes cooked to mush on the stove. I remember thinking that this wasn't supposed to happen to Donna Ruth.

"What's the matter, honey?" Lydia's voice startled me. I turned to face the woman who helped Grandmother with spring cleaning. Lydia had come to offer her help, bringing along her handyman husband, Crack. He earned the nickname when, as a child on a camping trip, he survived a lightning strike.

Lydia always startled me because her eyes and manner were exactly like Momma's. Now, as she repeated her question, she sounded like Momma too, making my tears flow again.

"It's okay, Donna Ruth, I'm here now, I'll help you. Sh-h-h!" And the knowing mother of seven children held me and sensed the depth of my pain without guessing its cause.

At the end of the week, the minister's son gave me a ride home. Paul was a friend now; his sisters invited me to their home whenever I visited my grandparents. A mature fourteen-year-old, he had been chauffeuring his father, who didn't drive, around Howard Lake for a couple of years. Lately he'd been driving to Minneapolis, too, and was going now to retrieve his father from a visit there. So far, the tall unlicensed boy and his genial immigrant father with the clerical collar had not been stopped by highway patrol officers. Nor by either of Howard Lake's deputies, who knew the boy's age.

We pulled up in front of my house in the 1936 Plymouth. Like many people, the pastor had been saving for a new model just as car production ceased so that Chrysler, Ford, and General Motors could make tanks, jeeps, and airplane engines.

"Do you, uh, go out on dates at all?" I knew and liked Paul well enough that his question didn't surprise me.

"Well, just a movie or skating a couple of times."

"Do you ever go out with older guys?"

I laughed. "Not really, but my mother thinks your dad is a saint— so what does that make you?"

"Not too pious, I hope," he said, his brown eyes turning soft and just barely mischievous. He laid his hand over mine in a friendly gesture of farewell. I tried to block out the raw memory of Dean's hands, but the stress of holding the secret inside me was making me sick. I withdrew my hand abruptly.

"Is something wrong?" he asked, concerned.

"No, I'm just tired."

Mother was glad to see me; she had even bought me a present. When Paul left after a few polite minutes, I opened my gift, a cotton dirndl skirt and a white ruffled blouse for my remaining weeks of school. Then she was eager to hear about Grandmother's condition.

I knew she believed her mother was perfect, but I didn't know she feared that Grandmother was dying. I needed to talk about my own feelings from this arduous week, Grandmother's demands, maybe even Dean's abuse.

It came rushing out, "Grandmother was so mean and crabby—"

She reached over and slapped my face. "Don't you ever talk about her like that!"

Stung, I stepped up to her and cuffed her shoulder. "Don't ever hit me again," I said between clenched teeth, my eyes blazing with pent-up fury. Our warm reunion was over. I didn't share my hurts, and she didn't ever hit me again.

∾   ∾

We lost both grandmothers that summer. Grandmother Patrick died after an illness that kept Mother at her side for two weeks. When Mother gave me the unexpected news about Gram Scott, I went to the quiet bedroom to hug Dad. It was the first time I saw him cry.

Gram died at age ninety-four—of pneumonia—only two days after she had been following her normal routine. Her days all began with a brisk walk to the bakery for breakfast sweet rolls. If I stayed the night on Aunt Dorothy's couch, I'd walk with her, barely able to keep up with her small quick steps as I listened to her lively chatter.

"Did I tell you about that young fellow who offered to help me cross the street?"

"What did you tell him, Gram?" I wanted to hear her say it again.

"Sonny," she'd say, straightening her back, "I was crossing

streets long before your father was born, so I guess I should know how.''

After breakfast I'd help her weed and water her garden. She'd lean on the hoe, face shaded by her sunbonnet, looking like a little girl in a flowered dress that brushed her ankles above dainty slip-on shoes bought in the children's department.

Aunt Dorothy's marriage the year before, when she was forty-nine, had forced her retirement from the telephone company after many years as a supervisor. Uncle Oscar, a widower, took Dorothy and her mother into his two-story home next door to the church where he and Dorothy met. Gram would have everyone believe that Oscar's teasing annoyed her. Actually he (a bedeviling hulk nearly four times Gram's ninety pounds) was the perfect foil for her crusty independence. She always seemed to get the last word.

"What's gotten into you today?" Uncle Oscar would ask her. "You're like a bear with a sore paw."

She'd glance pointedly from his head to his feet and back again. "Look who's calling who a bear!" she'd say, huffing off to her next project.

⌒ ⌒

Mother, before marriage ended her career, was an extraordinary nurse. From her, I heard stories of her escapades while she was a boarding student at St. Mary's Hospital in Minneapolis, receiving two dollars spending money every Saturday from her parents. She would spend half of it that day to buy two pairs of stockings and bring home a quart of ice cream and a small jar of chocolate syrup. She and her roommate Della would eat the ice cream quickly, topping it with peanuts Mother had sneaked from the baking kitchen downstairs. From this and other stories I could well imagine Laura Patrick as a young woman, fresh and hopeful, popular and funny.

I heard from others that, even before she earned her R.N. degree, she was earning praise from people who received her attentive care. Those who worked beside her valued her professional skill too, but even more they appreciated the personal interest she showed in each of them, including those who wore the black and white habit of the Order of the Sisters of St. Joseph.

After Pat and I were on our own, she would recertify, rejoin the staff at St. Mary's, and quickly become a head nurse. And a few years after that, at the hospital's fiftieth anniversary celebration, she would be named its "Nurse of the Half Century." That singular honor recognized her loving care for patients and their families, combined with reliability, infallibility, and all the other abilities the hospital desired in its nurses. There was also the glamour of her return to demanding work, still lovely and capable in her fifties, a rare and notable accomplishment then. There may even have been a few votes from physicians who were impressed by her unquestioning deference to doctors (learned as a student nurse in the 1920s), an homage becoming passé as nurses' specialty education and salaries increased.

But for me, the real essence of her nursing skill was embodied in a story she told me one day. I was telling her about my new friend Joanne, and I saw a faraway look in her eyes. She told me she'd done some private-duty nursing during her training. A young patient named Joanne suffered from a terminal disease. The girl's mother had left the family; her father had become wary and detached.

When Mother became alarmed about her patient's worsening condition, she planned an early birthday celebration. She baked a cake for Joanne, with nine candles stuck into marshmallows, then bought a present, a telescope, with her own meager funds and persuaded the father to sign the card. That evening, when the excited girl couldn't sleep, Mother bundled her in a blanket and took her to the porch to sing to her in the moonlight.

The next afternoon, Joanne died in Mother's arms after telling her, "Say good night to the stars for me."

⌒ ⌒

The country was in its fourth year of war when President Franklin Roosevelt died. His sudden fatal stroke left the country reeling. We would move into the concluding months of combat led by Harry Truman, a seemingly mild man from Missouri whom we barely knew.

Dad voted a straight Democratic Farmer Labor ticket. When there was no party affiliation to guide him, his decision was based on a candidate's surname. He would make out a list of his choices, and make a copy for Mother to take to the polls.

"This O'Brian must be Catholic," he'd tell her, "so be sure to vote for Johnson. This guy Golden is a sheeny, but he'd make a better judge than the woman running against him. Women are too emotional to be judges. That gal clerk they hired at the roundhouse cries every time you look at her."

When both candidates were equally unacceptable to him, because of party, religion, or gender, he'd have to resort to reading about their qualifications and experience—or at least their area of expertise. "This fella was a teacher, so he'd be better on the school board than the shyster." Dad's narrow views were all too common then, but seemed senseless to me. At the state school, with its racial and religious diversity, ethnic differences were overshadowed by our common plight. I didn't try to convince Dad. I noticed that Patrick, raised in this house, didn't buy into the stereotypes either, so I was sure the callous prejudgments would end with our generation.

We'd been studying in school about the suffragists. When Dad handed Mother her list, I thought Susan B. Anthony must be twirling in her grave. I went with Mother to the polling place, curious to see if all the women had lists. On the way, I lectured her.

"Do you know that women went to prison to get that franchise for you?"

"Yes, I know. Don't worry," she said, smiling, and closed the conversation with her humming.

Waiting in line, I noted with anger that many of the women carried slips of paper or had husbands whispering at their sides. My mother took her time over her ballot. The list remained in her purse.

⌒ ⌒

I was numbed by the maelstrom of death and destruction my country unleashed on Hiroshima and, three days later, Nagasaki. The two atomic bombs killed nearly 102,000 people and rained suffering on many thousands more. (Why do we speak of people dying "by the thousands" when we know they die individually—just as they live and love individually?) At my tender age, nearing thirteen, it seemed to me that just a clear threat of the hideous bomb would have accomplished the same thing. Japan, we'd been told, was "already on the ropes." Couldn't we have demonstrated its monstrous capability with a blast on an unoccupied island, I wondered? For sure, one bomb would have forced the same surrender.

My cousin Bill, stopping by our house, expressed his own regret over our retaliatory bombing.

"Do you think Roosevelt would have killed all those civilians, Uncle Lee?" he asked. Bill was fifteen and already planning to become a doctor. In fact, he would be in school and training many years, emerging as a pediatric cardiologist.

Dad was furious. "Don't you defend those dirty Japs!" he said. "The Bible says 'An eye for an eye.' "

"The Bible says 'Thou shall not kill,' " Bill said quietly.

My father was not used to challenges. He met this one as if questioning one of his certainties cast doubt on them all. He rose from his chair, ordered Bill to leave the house, and pushed the door hard behind him.

Upset at the banishment of the cousin I so admired, I stalked away muttering a few words of agreement with Bill's arguments. Dad stormed into my bedroom, raging.

"If you think you know more than me," he said, "you can pack your things and head back where we found you." It was the first time he had ever said "it."

Mother heard, too late to stop his words. I could hear her whispering harshly to him before she came in to comfort me. She must have expected uncontrollable sobs—the reaction she triggered with similar words a year ago. Instead she found a steely silence, the sound of something dying inside me. When her own tears of distress brought no response, she backed out of my bedroom with a soft "I'm sorry, sweetheart."

I preferred to believe she hadn't told him about our earlier scene. Either way, he didn't apologize, and because he didn't, it took me many years to forgive him.

⌒ ⌒

Patrick had moved into the newly heated and insulated attic. The back bedroom was mine. I could fall asleep to my radio, crying over ballads sung by Fran Warren or a young and innocent Frank Sinatra, or thumping my feet to nonsense songs—"Mairzy Doats" by the

Merry Macs or Freddy Martin's lively version of "The Hut-Sut Song." I knew all the popular lyrics and sang incessantly around the house. Mother enjoyed it more than the male householders did, but Dad never complained until he heard me belting out a Harold Arlen/Johnny Mercer song called "Blues in the Night" from a recording by Ella Mae Morse.

"Snooks!" Dad's stern tone got my attention. "I don't want to hear that song in this house again," he said. His order gave the song's words more importance than they had before:

> My momma done told me, when I was in pigtails,
> My momma done told me, Hon,
> A man is a two-face,
> A worrisome thing who'll leave you to sing
> The blue-hoose in the ni-hight!

I'd found Dad's core of sensitivity: anything derogatory to men. Thereafter, I sang it loudly when I was alone, and under my breath when he was around. I got better and better at my solo performance, adding some finger snaps, loose hip movements, and facial contortions, until I could have taken it on the ro-hoad!

⇝ ⇜

My tall, handsome brother graduated from high school, vice president of his class, in June of 1946. I loved and admired him, and felt that he respected and cared about me. But we each had our own agenda: Pat struggled to attain the self-reliance that was requisite in our family, while I groped for bits of praise to bolster my self-esteem. I'm not sure we knew, then, how to help each other.

Early in the afternoon of Pat's graduation day, I walked home from school alone. Usually Luanne and Patricia walked with me until we took different directions two blocks from my house. Today they had left in family cars to go out for treats after our own junior high graduation, a brief low-key program that half the parents, including mine, did not attend. Both of my friends had invited me along, but I'd promised to help with Pat's graduation dinner.

I knew I'd find Mother in a preparty panic, fussing over dishes that would ultimately taste delicious and look like works of art. She had won the most canning ribbons at the State Fair for two years straight but still couldn't relax about entertaining.

Our guests that night would include Granddad, all the aunts, uncles, and cousins, Pat's godparents (Sara Branch and her husband, Fred, a Great Northern Railroad locomotive engineer), and Pat's girlfriend—about eighteen of us. It would be Bill's first visit since the scene in our living room, nearly a year ago. Bill had apologized to Dad—not, he stressed, for his convictions—but "if I showed any disrespect for you."

"Hello, Donna Ruth," our neighbor Mrs. Ranallo called as I neared home. She squinted at me in the bright sun. "You look so pretty today."

"Thank you," I said, shifting the bag of miscellaneous cleared from my desk over to the other arm.

I felt my sheer white blouse sticking to my back. The pleated skirt in fuchsia and teal plaid was too warm for this day, although the wool was a soft lightweight challis. Maybe I shouldn't have worn this new outfit today. Would I have time to launder the blouse for tonight? And I should curl my drooping hair.

Nylon stockings trapped moist heat on my legs, and unfamiliar garters irritated my thighs as I walked. Often that day, I'd admired the new T-strap sandals that flattered my small nyloned feet; now I could hardly wait to kick off the shoes and rub my cramped toes.

But as I approached our house, the scent from the fairy rose bush drifted to meet me. I loved to wear its shell-pink blossoms in my hair. I thought how familiar this house seemed now, and how the word *familiar* was so like *family*.

Mother was waiting for my well-trained assistance. I put on shorts and hung my rinsed and dripping blouse on the line, then snipped flowers—iris and lacy wood fern—for the tables. I carved radishes into tulips, as Mother had taught me, and dropped them into ice water.

Later, while I ran a tub and brushed my teeth, ignoring Pat's complaints from the other side of the locked bathroom door, I frowned at my reflection. No time to revive limp hair now; maybe a quick touch-up in the bedroom, after I ironed my blouse.

"Pat, would you grab my blouse off the line? Oh, and plug in the iron."

"Who was your servant last year?"

"Be nice, and I promise not to spill gravy on your new jacket tonight."

"Just be out of there by the time the iron's hot, or the blouse will be branded. The old Iron Triangle Ranch brand."

Each graduate of Pat's large class was allotted just four admission tickets to Edison High School's auditorium unless more were needed to seat their parents and siblings. I was carefully pressing my fragile blouse when Mother told me the plans for tonight's ceremony: Mother, Dad, Aunt Mary, and Aunt Dorothy would use our tickets. Bill and I were to sneak in through the usher's entrance and try to find standing room in the balcony.

"If anyone stops you," Pat coached us, "tell them Mr. Liemohn sent you."

I could tell it was useless to protest the arrangement; Mother had the notion that the two aunts should represent the recently deceased grandmothers. I felt my face flush with humiliation. Even in that era, so totally dominated by adults, this was an unusual affront that would embarrass me in front of my peers, many of whom would be there to applaud their own brothers and sisters. Worse, it made me wonder if I would ever have full membership in this family.

As it happened, the man to whom Bill and I lied at the door was Mr. Liemohn himself. I suspected, from the way he raised his thick eyebrows and paused before he waved us through, that the tall, distinguished-looking gentleman was the Usher's Club adviser. I learned for sure when I walked into his math class three months later, on my first day at Edison High.

In between dinner and the ceremony, Pat hurriedly opened gifts—a Bulova watch from our parents, a silver tie bar from his date, a record album from me, and a stack of cards with five- and ten-dollar bills. I received a graduation present too—a box with two silver charms for my bracelet—from Pat and his steady girlfriend Marilyn.

☞ ☜

Right after his graduation, Pat enlisted in the army. He was eager to escape his father's house and determined to earn a college education under the G.I. Bill. He'd had jobs since he was very young, but he had used his money for "nonessential" clothes, gasoline when he was allowed to borrow the Graham-Paige, and of course for the dates he squeezed between school and work hours.

On at least one occasion that I knew of, he and some buddies made a beer run over the border to Wisconsin, where the drinking age was lower. Pat stashed a leftover bottle in our refrigerator. Mother promptly poured it down the drain.

When Pat left for boot camp, I missed his young presence and wrote to him often but felt quite confident of his safety. World War II had ended a year before, and the Korean conflict would erupt after his discharge.

Mother, however, was terrified. Pat was assigned to the Eighty-second Airborne Division, and Mother had daily visions of him jumping out of an airplane wearing a faulty parachute. She became so irritable and depressed that Dad eased his demands on her and tried, unsuccessfully, to cajole her out of her black mood. She seemed so miserable, I thought she might also be suffering some delayed reaction to her mother's death. In fact, at age forty-seven, she could have been enduring symptoms of menopause. If so, she referred to it only obliquely, choosing pride over sympathy.

I felt sad, seeing her despair; it reminded me of tearful Momma the day she brought my doll Jane to Owatonna, the day her trembling voice couldn't read Grandma's card. A shock wave hit me: Was Momma distraught over her son that day? Had she just learned of Duane's pending adoption? Letting go of a beloved son must be painful whatever the circumstances.

Jane. I hadn't thought about her for a while. It was as if she belonged to a different life.

chapter

ten

Branching Out

I still thought about Yvonne. Not daily, as I had after we were parted, but in response to random memory triggers: a pink hairbrush, apples fallen from a tree, a mention of July 11—her birthday. I scrutinized grainy newspaper photographs of anyone named Yvonne who could be about two years my senior, looking to see if she rimpled her chin when she posed for a picture. A girl the right age— by any name—drew my attention if she had my nose and mouth in a narrower face. I knew my sister would be scouting for signs of me, too, wherever she was.

My thoughts of her became increasingly chimeric in proportion to my advancing adolescence. I would envision us—an accidental meeting aboard a ship or in an airport (I'd never been either place)— recognizing each other instantly. We would embrace, amid flashbulbs and cheers, and walk away arm in arm, promising to share sisterly secrets. (Of course, both of us now pronounced our sibilants perfectly.)

Adolescent changes also might have magnified the turmoil erupting inside me, the grief about my past—the losses, abuses, insecurities. I tried to ignore those feelings (I was becoming too good at denying feelings), but sometimes it was like trying to disregard an elephant in the living room.

Sometimes, in the dark, thoughts of my secret past dragged me down into the place where all the pain lay hidden. A place with handcuffs, a screen, and—always—a courtroom. Or the feel of bruising hands under a gray blanket, or an image of Patty sitting alone at a table, her chin held high above a plate of cold liver until Yvonne could sneak by and jam the odorous meat into her pocket.

I had thought the wad of decaying feelings stuffed deep inside would seem smaller as I grew, but it seemed to grow with me, picking up bits of every disappointment, coloring my perception of people's motives. Did a certain relative look directly at my brother but always over my head because he didn't know how to talk to young girls? Or because he still didn't consider me a real member of the family, worthy of his attention? Did the mother of a friend, telling me I was lucky to have gotten such nice parents, intend to compliment my family? Or to portray me as a poor little bastard, rescued from the depths of sin and sadness?

And what was the matter with me that I couldn't just forget about it all, as I'd been told to do?

One night, trying to shut down my thoughts and sleep, I felt overwhelmed with pain and sadness. There was a hole in my stomach; my feet were touching electric current. Dad had left for work, but I hadn't heard Mother go to bed. I would go to her, let the tears come, tell her I felt troubled, injured, defiled. Tell her I needed someone to acknowledge my pain—or convince me it wasn't real.

A force outside myself propelled me from my bed to the dark dining room. I stood there on bare feet. The door to the kitchen was propped open. The bulb over the sink shed pale light over my mother, seated on the wooden bench of the breakfast nook. Her arms formed a circle on the table, cushioning her head, while her shoulders moved in the jerky rhythm of barely audible sobs.

I stood watching for a moment, too drained to move, wondering which of her disappointments had caught up with her tonight.

I still needed for her to hear me, lead me back to bed, talk to me, rub my back. But the possibility of rejection was something I couldn't risk right now. Feeling like a spy, I watched a moment longer, considered going to comfort her. Then I turned away and walked silently back to my room.

⤙ ⤚

Mother's "total blue funk," as I referred to it with my close friends, lasted about three months into my freshman year. Then, though still prone to mood swings, she became more interested in my activities, excited about Christmas. At the time it puzzled me. Now I wonder if Pat's departure made her aware I would leave someday too.

She was pleased when I made the intramural all-star field hockey team and then, overcoming my small size with speed and tenacity, the basketball all stars. Girls could not participate in prep sports against other schools, except as cheerleaders (and I learned that limber girls who wore glasses needn't apply), but the six or eight gym classes in our grade competed against each other, then chose the top players from all the teams for a final championship game.

I expected Mother to dismiss these sports as unladylike, but she brought out an old photograph of her own basketball team—wearing white middy blouses and dark woolen bloomers, Mother's long hair caught back in a large black bow—and laughingly compared it to my team in our white shirts and navy blue cuffed shorts.

Mother's high school days had included interscholastic sports for girls. Then, strangely, in 1939 the Minnesota Department of Education outlawed "stressful" competition for girls. The ban would not be lifted until 1970. To my disappointment, gymnastics training was not offered to girls either, except in dainty doses, just enough to pass our "fitness tests."

One day, I was rummaging in the attic crawl space next to Patrick's empty bedroom. An old trunk held bits and pieces of my parents' past: photographs, a lace shawl, bone china plates, Pat's baby book. I could see, far back in the corner, the edge of a white box under a pile of rag rugs. I pulled it out, opened it—and there was Jane! Sturdy Jane, smaller than I remembered her, but calm, with her trusting look. I was surprised, relieved that my parents hadn't destroyed her. Then

I thought of her here, all along, close yet hidden, while the child me longed for her. My conflicting emotions flowed back and forth with a rocking motion that sickened my stomach.

I didn't dare take her downstairs; it might anger Dad into disposing of her, or send Mother into another tailspin. Instead, I paid her daily visits in the stuffy corner beneath the sloping ceiling. Each time, I replaced her carefully in the box, hating myself for conforming to their secrecy, until I realized that she was no longer able to comfort me as she had once comforted Patty.

＝ ＝

Dad had every Saturday and Sunday night off now. He had benefited from the growing strength of labor unions (and Henry Ford's revolutionary "trickle up" theory: "Pay workers enough so they can buy cars"). But his hip was deteriorating, causing him to count the months until his retirement—still more than a hundred months away.

And he remained intolerant of change or challenge.

My father didn't believe women should wear pants. Like the net "snoods" to keep long hair in place, pants had been popularized by women working in defense plants—women who had won recognition in the hit song "Rosie the Riveter" recorded by the Andrews Sisters. Dad grudgingly permitted my jeans (allowed in school only on football game Fridays), and my slacks and shorts for sport wear, but he made it clear he wouldn't tolerate "men's clothes" on Mother.

She bought a lovely wool outfit, ski pants and a matching jacket in a raspberry shade, with embroidered pink flowers and green leaves around the collar and down the front. She wore it sometimes on errands or outings with me, then hung it away at the back of the hall closet, behind the vacuum cleaner, where Dad never looked. I thought it was a shame he never saw his tall slim wife in that sexy outfit.

Mother's acquiescence to his demands was one of the things she and I still argued about. ("Rosie" had gingerly bent some gender roles too.) "I'll never dance to some guy's tune like that," I'd tell her angrily.

"Then you'll dance alone," she'd say, in a tone that implied a fate worse than incarceration.

I began to think a lot about what type of man I preferred. On Dad's night off, I still went sometimes to a movie with my parents.

Dad would only go to films that had one-dimensional heroes like Humphrey Bogart (his favorite) or Gary Cooper. He preferred foreign intrigue or westerns. But, with my girlfriends, I lusted after leading men like Cary Grant and Dana Andrews—romantic, debonaire, witty men. I'd read that, during the Renaissance, European men were expected to be multifaceted. Athletes were not excused from social graces, intellect, and neatness; scholarly men were obliged to maintain physical fitness and display warmth and humor. Wasn't that still a reasonable expectation?

Petite girls like me benefited from boys' prevailing preference to date girls shorter than they were. But the ranks of short boys dwindled, every month it seemed; growth spurts overtook them as quickly as whiskers popped from their chins. Meanwhile, I learned to appreciate the special qualities of several boys—a small gymnast, a violin virtuoso, a funny-by-nature math whiz—I might have overlooked if I'd been a long-legged beauty competing for the popular jocks.

Now that mother had relaxed about me a little (apparently deciding that my blossoming figure would attract a husband despite my untamed mouth and arrogance about men), I seemed to have become expert at irritating Dad.

He objected to my taking German because he hated "the krauts." Mother convinced him I needed a language in order to get into nurse's training. I had no intention of becoming a nurse; the sight of blood made me weak. The truth was, my A's in junior high English allowed me to enroll in a two-year language class as a freshman (with all those junior boys!).

To my close friends Luanne, Patty, and Joanne, my German class added another. Her name, Ruth, was one that kept cropping up importantly in my life. I liked Ruthie's unaffected ease, not common in girls our age. She was smart, loyal, and had a sense of humor that was, like mine, a little offbeat.

We talked on the phone in a fractured pidgin German we made up, glossing over any unknown term by using an English word with a German prefix:

"Wo bist du gegoing dieser Abend?" I'd ask.

"Ich bin zu die Kirche gegangen."

"Ach, du bist eine guten Luteran Fraulein."

Our conversations no doubt amused Ruthie's mother, who caught the gist of them because her first language was Swedish, but they frustrated the bejeezus out of Dad. I insisted we had to practice in order to succeed in class, so he'd fume in silence until finally he'd snap "That's enough!" and I'd revert to English.

"Gotta go, Ruthie. See you tomorrow." No matter how innocuous our conversation was, it felt satisfying to keep a little of it private, sitting there at the phone table by the dining room archway, just twelve feet from Dad's chair.

Dad was increasingly critical of my clothes. Because I had few, I improvised. I cut off slacks that had become too short (and probably too tight) and made cropped tops from old blouses, removing the sleeves and tying the tails above my midriff.

He even belittled the free golf lessons I received from Luanne's father. "Cow pasture pool!" Dad snorted, ignoring my reminder that his revered Scottish forebears had invented the game.

Dad was vigilant about boyfriends too. They were really just pals, part of a group that held parties in our unfinished basements, dancing to phonograph records. But Dad wanted to know their last names. (If it was a surname I knew he wouldn't vote for, I'd make one up.) Even my reading angered my father now. He'd see me stretched out with a book and say, "Don't you have anything better to do? Go help your mother."

So I was relieved, the summer after my freshman year, when Aunt Mary invited me to their farm for a week. My cousins Vernon and Richard had returned now from overseas service and attended the University of Minnesota. Their sister Mary would be starting her senior year at Augsburg College in Minneapolis. They planned to detassel Uncle Charlie's acres of commercial seed corn, and I could help. They told me from which rows I should pull the pollen-bearing flowers, although no one completely explained the purpose to me.

The week was exhausting—everyone worked hard all day—but affirming too. The family gathered around the piano in the small farmhouse every evening to play instruments and sing hymns: "Oh, come to the church in the wildwood . . ." I took a lot of teasing from Uncle Charlie and my cousins for my "city ways," but Aunt Mary made sure I got my turn.

"Now, Donna Ruth, you just tell them they don't know everything. Did Charlie tell you about the time he drove the wrong way down a one-way street in Minneapolis—then went around the block and did it again?''

On my first day back home, Dad rushed me to his overgrown garden, then he dashed home for some reason. I was determined to get back on his good side. When he returned, I had just finished my surprise—detasseling his sweet corn.

''What on earth have you done?'' he asked, staring. ''Did you pull the tassels off all that corn?''

''Sure. That's how they get better hybrids or something on the farm.'' I gave him my best aw-shucks grin, still not realizing that my good deed would prevent this corn from maturing, that with no male tassels the female silks could not be pollinated. The complexity of Uncle Charlie's selective crossbreeding was far over my head.

Dad looked again at the stunted stalks and mentally kissed good-bye the plump buttery ears of his favorite crop. Then he laughed, so hard and long I thought he'd fall off his two canes.

꒰ ꒱

A few weeks into my sophomore year, a sweet boy from the junior class whom I barely knew stopped by my locker to stammer an invitation to the homecoming dance. I declined; he kept asking. Seeing no line form to take his place, I accepted a couple of days before the dance. There I learned he was an excellent dancer (my first experience with a lead strong enough to follow), and I noticed that many of the girls who attended the informal affair without dates watched us with envy.

Ben and I dated until spring, mostly house parties and other dances. He was thoughtful and undemanding, and he introduced me proudly to his nice circle of friends. Suddenly I broke it off, rudely, with no explanation because there was none. I only knew I felt like I was suffocating, weighted down with that familiar feeling of obligation. Maybe it was simply that I hadn't chosen him. This time, I wanted to get to choose.

All his loyal friends avoided me after that. But for several weeks I'd see Ben, sad and sulking, watching me. I fervently wished he'd find a lovely girl, one who would appreciate him. My concern for him faltered, just a little, the day I saw her clinging to his arm.

As soon as I turned fifteen, tired of baby-sitting for twenty-five cents an hour, I lied a year onto my age and applied for a job, for a dime an hour more, at the S&L (Salkin and Linoff) department store. I was elated when Mr. Rock, the personnel manager, phoned to tell me I was hired. In my family, to earn a paycheck was to exchange total impotence for a measure of independence, a smidgen of power. A job! It would free me from many dreary home chores and give me money of my own.

I worked Saturdays and the two weeknights the store stayed open late. One Monday evening, alone in the sportswear department, I folded and sized a long table full of blouses and stacked them in even rows. There was not one customer on the second floor, so I stepped over to talk to the saleswoman in lingerie.

Verna would have been tall even without the ankle-strap platform shoes she always wore. I tried to imagine her without heavy makeup, almost certain that her investment of time and money were counter-productive.

I preferred to wear little or no makeup, now that I could decide. At the moment, I felt fresh and pretty in my favorite outfit. A crisp white shirt collar peeked above my sweater, an argyle pattern in white, tan, and forest green. My tan gabardine pleated skirt ended maybe ten inches above shined loafers. Mother had told me I looked "professional," so I tied a dark green ribbon in front of my long hair.

Now, with Verna draped over the counter, taking weight off one tired foot, I smiled at the picture we must present. She with her dark-rimmed eyes and flashy clinging clothes. Gidget meets Mata Hari. Suddenly our supervisor was at my elbow. (I've managed to forget his name but not his stern, ruddy face.) Usually, his body odor preceded him.

"Why aren't you working?" he asked me.

I looked around to see if a customer had escaped my notice. "There is no more to do," I said.

He stomped over to the tidy sale table and windmilled both hands through rows of blouses until they were thoroughly mixed.

"Well, now there is," he said, pursing his lips in a sick smile. "And when you've finished, come to my office."

I sorted the mess, with a little help from Verna, who worked slowly, trying not to impale the blouses on her stiletto fingernails.

Then, more fearful than angry, I went to his small office down the hall. He stood and motioned me to close the door. He had removed his suit jacket; his tie was loosened now, and his shirttail was half out. He appeared friendly, and reached out to shake my hand.

"I hope you understand. We can't have customers come in and see you idle." His voice was different but I was too relieved to care.

"Yes sir, I understand." The hand he offered me felt warm and sticky. His left hand, on its way to my shoulder, brushed upward across my breast. An accident?

"You can stay here awhile—it's not busy tonight," he said. His face grew redder and he took a step closer. I looked up into eyes that were moist, hooded.

I tried to free my hand but he whipped his head down and put his mouth completely over mine, his tongue poking at my clamped lips. I shook my shoulders and spun loose. While I stumbled to the door, wiping my mouth, he said, "Little girl, you got a lot to learn."

I hurried to the employee lounge. There I scrubbed my hands and face, rinsed my mouth, and listened, terrified, for a sound from the hallway. In the mirror, my frightened face stared back at me, with puffy lips, the pupils of my eyes like pin dots in the glaring light.

Back on the sales floor, I mechanically counted out my cash drawer. From a cubbyhole under the counter I pulled my old jacket, then carefully lifted my soft brown purse, remembering how happy I was when I retrieved it from lay-by with my most recent paycheck. I choked with sadness, too tense and knotted for tears. From my swamp of feelings, two predominated: a sense of injustice that he could take away my joy and a fear that I had drawn his attention somehow—perhaps by my manner. Or maybe my earlier loss of innocence was as obvious as Verna's flaming rouge.

In the descending elevator Verna asked me, "What did old Stinky want?"

"Whatever he could get," I said, hardly recognizing my tight dry voice.

She laughed and said, "That old goat! He paws anything that moves."

I was shocked at her casual attitude toward something that felt so hurtful and wrong. At the same time, I welcomed this idea of random victims. Was this true? Were there men who did these things haphazardly, willy-nilly, without any provocation or cause?

I didn't tell my parents. I was afraid they'd make me quit my job—and even more afraid that they wouldn't.

If Patrick had been home, I might have sought his advice, but I couldn't write such a letter. I remembered those wartime billboards urging us to "keep up the morale of our fighting men."

In my bed that night, I battled confusion. I knew this unattractive man had a wife; I'd waited on her in the store, a soft smiling woman. Their son had been at her side, an awkward boy who wore his red hair parted down the middle like his father's and studied his shoes a lot.

Normally, in bed, I sprawled on my stomach with arms raised, lobster-style, and one arm hooked around my pillow, as if I feared that a matron would come to take it away. But tonight I lay on my back, trying to forget his sour breath, while tears rolled down past the tops of my ears. I felt alone, my body rigid and unclean even after a long bath. This violation seemed even worse than the others. Because I was older? Forced to consider various responses, however much I wanted to obliterate the memory?

I fell asleep while I was trying to pray. Before I drifted off, I had a strange sensation of rising off the bed in peaceful suspension, hands supporting my back, filling me with a silent message: "It's all right, Patty. It's all right."

The next day the problem was still there. I woke with a heavy feeling of dread and rose quickly to leave the demons behind. Maybe I should tell Mr. Rock, the kindly Lincolnesque man who had hired me. Would he believe me? Call my parents? Tell the child welfare people?

I tried again to put it out of my mind. I found myself unexpectedly embarrassed at the prospect of telling Ruthie, or other friends I assumed were sheltered and innocent. Instead I chose a confidante I believed to be more worldly-wise (or just disenchanted like me?). Sylvia's solemn face had the strong features of her Slovakian ancestors. There was something defiant about her. I admired the way her proud carriage overcame the faded hand-me-downs she wore.

She and I shared a double desk in study hall. I knew her family was large and poor, her home more humble than mine. Sylvia waited tables in a café/bar near school.

"Syl, can I ask you a personal question?"

"Sure," she said, but her look was wary.

"Do boys—or men—ever come on to you?"

She looked down at me carefully. "You mean—force themselves on you?"

"Yeah, I guess." This was a mistake, I thought. She'll think I'm a pig.

"Sure, all the time," she said in a level tone just tinged with sadness.

Relieved, I pressed on. "What do you do about it?"

Her laugh was mirthless, but she touched my shoulder. "Don't ever let someone else define who you are—especially someone who doesn't care about you." She recited it like a creed. I repeated the words, memorizing them because they made my heart leap. The advice, she told me, had come from a priest.

"But," I still wanted to know, "how does that keep a guy from bothering you again?"

"The truth is," she said slyly, "I never have to worry about repeaters. My four brothers see to that."

My part-time job barely left time for homework, and too few hours for Ruthie, Luanne, and other friends. I hoped to be excused from Sunday night youth meetings at our Methodist church. Mother wouldn't hear of it.

How I hated being called on to confess my sins and accept Jesus as my Savior, in front of the entire coed class. I was afraid there must be something radically wrong with me because I had few sins on my conscience (surely none I cared to broadcast), and I wasn't convinced anyone had done a great job of shepherding my life so far. My cynicism aside, our leaders seemed satisfied only when the confession was accompanied by tears of remorse and relief. It embarrassed me to hear the others; it frightened and confused me that I couldn't conform.

Yet Mother's pretense of conformity also bothered me. Our minister railed against jewelry, movies, dancing—so many things that mother privately enjoyed. She did not object to my playing cards, even after our pastor warned that it would lead to gambling. I remember the sermon because it seemed silly to me.

". . . and God will *punish* the owners of bars who do the work of the devil and use red and white checkered cloths on their card tables."

He told us that lonely men walking by on the street would see the tablecloth that reminded them of home and be drawn into the bar, where "they will accept the evils of drink and gambling, and condemn their souls for eternity!"

"Amen. Yes, Brother!" the men in the front rows responded. I felt that Dad's absence from church was less hypocritical than Mother's feigned acceptance of the church's strict values.

Sometimes I went with Ruthie to youth activities at Gustavus Adolphus Lutheran Church—sleigh rides and campfires with songs and sharing. Even the leaders were not too intense to smile. I asked Mother if I could join that church. She knew that a boy in Luther League had caught my eye, so she suspected my motive was more secular than sacred. But, always happy to see me have boyfriends, she actually considered it, until her fear of our pastor overpowered her romantic nature.

Still, I was alert to her hesitation—the opening I needed. I told her I planned to attend Ruthie's church sometimes on Sunday mornings. She let the comment pass, preferring to make it my decision if Dad, or her pastor, asked.

The love I found there was not the sort my mother envisioned. Pastor Reuben Ford spoke, on my first visit, on the message of Ephesians 2:8 (to this day my favorite verse and the basis of my personal belief). The minister repeated it in glad and certain tones: "For by grace you have been saved through faith; and this is not your own doing, it is the gift of God."

In my years of hearing sermons and studying for confirmation, I had felt indoctrinated with the solemn and immense task of earning God's love. Now here it was, offered freely. My response, then, could come from joy and love, not fear and obligation!

A gift? As pure and unconditional as Esther Jenson's candy? And it was meant for *me*? Hallelujah!

Owatonna state school administration building *(photo by Frank T. Wilson; courtesy the Minnesota Historical Society)*

Cottage five, one of the "girls' cottages" *(photo courtesy the Minnesota Historical Society)*

(above) The state school playground (photo courtesy the Minnesota Historical Society)

State school monument, dedicated July 3, 1993

(above and left)
State school exhibit
in Owatonna

Patricia and Yvonne Pearson, ages seven and nine, at the orphanage in 1940

Donna Ruth Scott on adoption day

Laura and Leonard Scott, Patrick at age thirteen, and Donna, age nine

Donna and Patrick with Podunk

Grandmother and Granddad Patrick on their fiftieth anniversary

Gram Scott working in her garden

Luanne and Donna *(right)*, almost sweet sixteen, 1948

Donna and Glenn in 1948

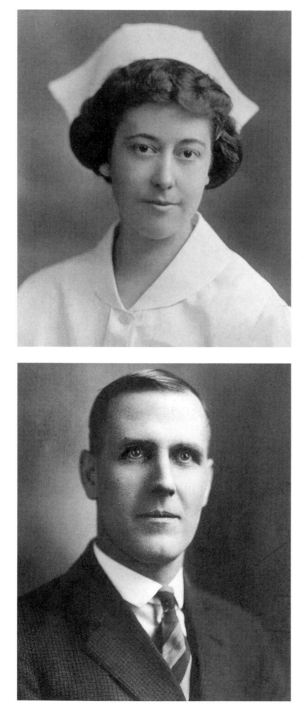

Laura Patrick as a
young nurse

Leonard Scott as a
young man

Laura Scott after she
returned to nursing,
1950

Leonard Scott, railroad foreman *(left)*, and machinists

Glenn and Donna in 1995

chapter eleven

Rain and Roses

My blind date bounded up to our front door in a downpour, my first clue that he would be different from boys my age. They'd have used the rain as an excuse to stay at the curb, honking the car horn. And he actually conversed with my mother—not just a nod and a mumble—then took my umbrella and covered me while I picked my way, in open-toed shoes, around the widening puddles. His own head, more than eight inches above mine, was at the mercy of wind and water. Luckily, the stiff pompadour wave in masculine vogue then was almost indestructible.

In the car, the two guys, his cousins, teased him:

"Hey, Captain Gallant!"

"Sir Walter, you forgot to lay down your coat." Their dates laughed, but Glenn showed no discomfort.

"You just can't hide class," he said.

That summer of 1948 I was still working at S&L, grateful that I'd had no reason to try to enlist the help of Sylvia's brothers. The next time old Stinky had approached me, I was forewarned by my nose (only slightly less sensitive than Mother's). I stepped behind some boxes I was unloading, then turned to face him. The words of Sylvia's priest pounded in my head; I stared up at him, my jaw set, with a look intended to say "I'm in control."

He looked at his shoes. For a moment, I glimpsed a man as insecure as his own gangly son. Then he cleared his throat.

"You're a good worker," he said. "If you want to work full time after school is out, it's okay by me." I nodded. He smiled wanly and then left.

On lunch breaks at work I'd become friends with Dolly, a classmate I'd barely known at school. Dolly's home was a troubled one, and her steady boyfriend David (a recent Edison graduate) was emotionally supportive. He had a reputation as a prankster, even a bit of a show-off. Actually, David relished a good joke, whether at someone else's expense or his own.

Earlier that July week of my blind date, Dolly was looking for two girls for a triple date on Saturday. The male trio would be Dave, his cousin Glenn (nearly eighteen like Dave), and another cousin, Ron, three years older. When I agreed to go (the plan was Excelsior Amusement Park), Dolly asked which of Dave's two cousins I'd prefer. Had I known it was a decision that would affect more than one evening, I might have asked more than one question.

"Which of these dudes is better looking?" I asked. Dolly considered, her head wagging that it was nearly a toss-up, then gave me her opinion.

"Then I'll take the other one," I said. "I'm sick of guys who are stuck on themselves."

When the evening arrived, Dolly had paired conventional Ron with her own kooky cousin (a match that proved to be as successful as mixing a fox and a hound), and the rain forced a change from the amusement park to a movie: *Key Largo*, with Lauren Bacall and Humphrey Bogart. We arrived at the ornate State Theater in midfilm and picked our way to three separate pairs of empty seats in the side balcony.

When we left the theater, again with the film in progress, I discovered that my new scarf was missing. Glenn convinced an unwilling usher to search our area with his flashlight until he located the scarf.

"Nice guy," I thought. I was sure my fifteen- and sixteen-year-old peers would have shrugged helplessly at my loss and walked on.

Glenn's maturity was even more evident when he good-naturedly ignored once more the "Sir Galahad" taunts from his comical cousin while Ron, now silent, drove us to a diner.

For the rest of the summer, Glenn or Dave would often beg their family car to drive Dolly and me home after work. My tired legs welcomed these respites from the streetcar ride and the four-block walk to my house. We'd stop at a drive-in for frosty mugs of Hires root beer, knowing David would do his best to keep us entertained. When his supply of jokes and stories ran out, he'd toss the carhop's dime tip into a glass of water ("Let her dive for it") or pretend to drive off with the tray still attached to the car window ("Let's see how fast she can run").

It was hard to reconcile these moments of insolence with his respectful, sensitive response to Dolly's family problems. He was her lifeline, and she seemed to disarm and stabilize him with her own self-effacing humor, so quick-witted but unfailingly kind. Again, as with Sally, it touched me to see a girl with pain and uncertainty in her own life bringing cheer and warmth to others.

⌒ ⌒

Patrick returned home with his honorable discharge and little choice but to return to his upstairs bedroom while he pursued his goal: to earn a degree in sociology in three years. I felt almost shy, at first, with this man who had left as a boy.

Mother mistook reticence for rudeness the day after Pat's arrival. We'd had, of course, a gathering of the clan for his homecoming. Afterward, I washed mountains of dishes while Mother, always a night owl, kept Pat up talking long after Dad left for work. The next morning I dragged myself, stretching and sleepy, into the living room and plopped into a chair without speaking to Pat, who was already dressed and breakfasted.

"Aren't you even going to say good morning to your brother?" Mother said.

"Why do you think it's up to me to speak first?" I asked. I could tell by her expression that the question never would have crossed her mind, but she had no argument to give as I left the room.

My brother appeared at some family meals and studied in his room, his radio tuned to *Suspense!* or to *The Green Hornet*'s announcer declaring, "He hunts the biggest of all game—public *enemies*." Most of his time was spent at the university, the library, his part-time job, or pursuing another interest, his pretty new Irish girlfriend.

With the self-reliance of his army days still raw and habitual, Pat couldn't tolerate it now when Mother fawned over him. When he couldn't ignore it, he'd borrow one of Dad's put-downs to gain some distance. "Sweetheart," Mother would say, greeting him at the door, "what can I do to help you get ready for your date on time?"

"You can move out of my way," he'd say, his face tight with irritation and discomfort.

Pat would pay me fifty cents to run a tub and shine his shoes, or to iron a shirt. It was partly his way of helping me get the things I needed; he knew the money drill with Dad all too well. It was also a ploy to keep Mother from hovering, without sacrificing the personal help that eased his crowded schedule.

"You don't have to pay her to do those things," Mother would tell him. "She's your sister."

"That's right—she's not my slave," he'd say, on his way up the stairs.

"But you work hard for your money," she'd call up to his room, more agitated now.

"You're right again. It's my money," he'd say, banging a drawer shut to emphasize that the subject was closed.

In time, I would clearly see these episodes as Pat's attempts to loosen his emotional links—links that could safely be restored after he achieved independence—to a mother who adored him. But for now, alone in the kitchen, I ironed and hummed with a smug grin on my face.

⌒ ⌒

In the middle of one gorgeous fall week, Ruthie and I told our mothers we planned to skip school the following day. When they agreed to cover for us with the required phone calls and notes, we were surprised. Although why shouldn't they? We were mature high school juniors now, and straight-A students.

I still remember the incredibly free feeling of that day, of walking, leaping, twirling in the block-square treed park within sight of Ruthie's house. We talked about teachers, parents, brothers, boys, sex, *the future.*

We lay for a while on a bed of dry leaves, finding images in soft layers of clouds, the kind Amelia Earhart had called "little lamb clouds."

"Look, there's Mickey Mouse."

"Where?"

"Right there between the giant fish and Jimmy Durante's profile."

Suddenly Ruthie asked, "Have you ever thought of looking for your sister?"

"Of course," I said, making the decision right then, "but not until my adoptive parents are dead."

"Why not?" Ruthie asked, puzzled.

"Because it would kill them." I declared it like literal truth. Even the thought of their reaction to such treachery put knots in my chest. Was that all of it? Or was I protecting myself too? Going back could threaten the one shaky identity I had.

We devoured our picnic lunch, talking about Yvonne and Owatonna, and comparing our home situations. My friend's large brown eyes, turned down a little at the outer corners exactly like her mother's, held me in a warm gaze. She would listen, then murmur an answer.

I stopped short of telling her about the Owatonna janitor, or Bud, or even my S&L boss. Thoughts of them made me feel dirty, defenseless, guilty—and then angry because they could still make me feel those things. I didn't want her to see me as different, a victim— or worse, shameful.

Instead we talked about God and faith. My own faith had matured some, thanks to Pastor Ford's clear sermons. I understood now that the promise of grace had a faith requirement, to accept our dependence on Jesus Christ.

"Ruthie, how do we know what to leave in God's hands and what we have to do for ourselves?"

"Well, I guess God sends the Holy Spirit to guide us, and we try to listen and do what it tells us. Verstehen Sie?"

"Ja, aber ich verstehen nicht *das* Holy Spirit. What gender do you think 'it' is?"

"Hmmm. I never really thought about that."

"Well, I have. The Trinity is Father, Son, and Holy Ghost, right? The way God created the universe, there can't be a father and son relationship without a feminine presence in there somewhere."

"Ach du Lieber! Was eine serious Freundin!" She crumpled dry leaves over my head.

We talked for hours, until the cloud pictures ran together and the trees gave up more leaves to the quickening wind. Then we hugged good-bye at her house, and I walked and ran the four blocks to mine. I had not felt so peaceful for a long time.

Glenn was attending the Minnesota School of Business and working for a wholesale jeweler downtown. He wanted to cut out of class early Friday afternoon to meet me at the Edison football game. I told him I wanted to go with my friends; they had been pulling away from me since I started to tie up evenings with work and with him. We met after the game, though, and I was struck again by the contrast between him and my male peers. Not that they weren't nice guys; he just seemed to have evolved a little further.

"How hungry are you?" he asked, hanging my jacket on a hook while I slid into a booth at our favorite café.

"Oh, I could handle a chocolate milkshake." With a mile-and-a-half walk just to get to school in the morning, I had no problem staying around 105 pounds.

"I'm starving." (He always was.) "I need a sandwich." He pulled a bill and change from his pocket. "I've got $1.27. Why don't we get one of each and split them? That will leave half a buck for gas." How easily he shared the problem, and included me in the solution.

My feelings for him were becoming more complicated. This skinny kid with his toed-out inherited gait had been easy to dismiss when I reported back to Dolly after that first date: "Oh, he's really nice, but I could never be serious about him."

That was before I noticed how well his shoulders fit the impeccable sport shirts he wore, the sleeves rolled above forearms strong and sinewy from an earlier job, lifting cases of beer off trucks at Kinsey's Tavern. And it was before I noticed that his long upper body tapered to a twenty-nine-inch waist, uncommon enough that he had to splurge on custom-tailored trousers. Still, just approaching my sixteenth birthday, I had no intention of becoming serious about anyone. I continued to date others and wanted him to do the same. Yet there were times, listening to his rich, pleasing bass voice, that I couldn't help wishing we were a little older.

Mother adored Glenn. She knew his parents from Masonic Lodge activities and thought his father was handsome and charming. Even Dad couldn't object to a boyfriend whose father was a day foreman in St. Paul for the same railroad that employed Dad, a boy who sang in his (Protestant!) church choir. (Dad didn't suspect that another boy I was seeing was Catholic despite his Scandinavian surname.) Mother, in fact, went overboard, putting more importance on my pleasing Glenn than on his pleasing me. The danger in her message was clear enough to me that I told her I resented it. I might as well have been speaking in tongues. She was convinced that she was merely looking out for my best interests, counteracting my stubborn independence.

"What does Glenn think about that?" she'd ask of my decision to cut my hair or to join the staff of the school newspaper.

"Who cares?" I'd had practice in self-reliance at an early age. I wanted his friendship, for God's sake, not his supervision!

"You'll never attract a man with that attitude."

"I don't want a man who dictates my attitude."

Meanwhile, the subject of our controversy remained cool and considerate. His kisses were warm but not insistent. He actually seemed to be interested in my mind, my feelings, even learning something about my past. And gradually, behind his good humor and our tireless search for fun—by ourselves or in a boisterous group—I glimpsed a young man who needed acceptance and validation almost as much as I did.

In eighth grade, at the invitation of my brother's friend Marilyn, I had joined Job's Daughters, a social and service order for girls, under the sponsorship of the Masonic Lodge.

I was puzzled why they chose such a tormented biblical life as the inspiration for this organization. Studying for my initiation, I read the Book of Job. A few verses resonated somewhere deep; I wrote them in my diary:

> For there is hope for a tree, if it be cut down,
> that it will sprout again, and its shoots will not cease.
> Though its root grow old in the earth,
> and its stump die in the ground,
> yet at the scent of water it will bud
> and put forth branches like a young plant. (Job 14:7-9)

My strange affinity with trees and leaves apparently remained as strong as when I envied the Scandinavian oaks their migration to a safe place.

I found in "J.D." another group of friends, gathered from four high schools. With them, I pretended to be as normal as I presumed they all were. I had served as chaplain and now, in my junior year, was chairing the decorations committee for the Sno Ball. It would be my first formal dance.

Just as the festive preparations got under way, I broke up with Glenn.

"Donna Ruth," Mother called to my room, "come to the phone. He really wants to speak to you."

"Tell him I'm not home."

"He says he's coming over."

"I still won't be home!"

He'd broken a Friday night date with me, explaining that he had to attend a family function. "My folks really want me to be there," he'd said.

"Sure, I understand. Have a good time," I said, trying to be as agreeable as he always was.

"I doubt that. I'd much rather be with you."

The following Monday in gym class, I heard that a group of guys that included Dave had spent Friday night partying, driving, having a very good time. I asked Dolly if Glenn had been with them. She said he was. The girls who witnessed my reaction seemed amused. Oh great! I thought; they must believe I'm a possessive nitwit if he has to lie in order to shake me for a night. The ones who knew Glenn liked him. They could spot his easy respect for women.

But this time he had not respected me—or at least he hadn't trusted me with the truth. All the disillusionment that resided just below my shaky surface erupted with a fury that frightened me. I didn't know where it was coming from and I couldn't control it. The only thing I could control was my decision not to talk to him, not to risk being hurt again.

Glenn waited for me after school one afternoon. I heard he was there, so I left by another door. My friends were enjoying the drama; my mother was upset with me.

"You're being unreasonable," she said for the tenth time that week. "No man will put up with such treatment."

Yes, I was sure he'd split now that he'd seen this mean, tough side of me. But I'd found my anger, my pride, and I couldn't let go of them. I feared they'd be replaced with that powerless feeling I knew too well.

⌒ ⌒

Christmas vacation began. Glenn no longer called or tried to get messages to me. Doggedly, I kept working on the decorations for others to enjoy. The Sno Ball would be held just after the new year began.

My family had our usual quiet Christmas Eve. Earlier that day, Mother had haggled over a scrawny fir tree, coaxing the price down to seventy-five cents. Pat and I wound strings of lights around the tree, testing to find the one dead bulb that kept the whole series from lighting. Mother carefully unwrapped glass ornaments, exclaiming over each one. We added silver icicles until they dripped from every inch of the branches, then Mother fastened the star on top and pro-nounced it "the most beautiful tree we've ever had." It was all so predictable, and therefore reassuring.

Pat connected the track of his boyhood electric train set so it circled the tree stand. We pulled foil shreds from the boughs, laid them in front of the approaching train, and watched sparks shower over the track. We didn't care that we were too old for this play—it was Christmas.

Dad rose early for our dinner treat—Mother's homemade chow mein, her one acquired taste for a foreign dish. It was a strange holiday tradition for a Scotch-English-Irish family, but one that allowed Mother to sit down in the living room and enjoy the few hours before Dad left for work.

Mother played a few carols then. The piano that was mostly silenced by Dad's daytime sleeping now added as much warmth as the fire crackling in the grate.

Hearing her play, I thought about the piano lessons I'd given up after two years, partly because my practice hours were so restricted, partly because I disliked my teacher, our minister's wife. She was a humorless, pinch-faced woman, and my every mistake made her mouth twitch, as though she'd just bit into a lemon.

With patience, Mother kept trying to develop my musical talent, substituting voice lessons, which ended after two sessions. The man who gave me private lessons would coach my breathing with his hands on my diaphragm and upper chest. Even though he was proper and professional, his touch made me so anxious I told Mother simply that I hated it, and then quit.

I persisted in trying to find substitutes for sports, taking dance classes—ballet, acrobatic, and tap. For four years, I walked to class every Saturday counting the blocks (ten long ones, four short ones), and each spring Mother lent her limited sewing skills to the construction of my three recital costumes. I added baton lessons, intending to join the band when I got to high school. But they chose just two majorettes, both of whom had been twirling ever since they were tall enough for their child-size batons to clear the floor. One, in fact, already had her own row of little students.

Now, watching Mother's long graceful fingers over the keys, the contented smile on her face, I realized she had been trying to share her love of music with me. That I had rejected her attempts so abruptly must have hurt her. My early years had been mostly devoid of music; I simply didn't value it the way she did. I understood now that our separate past was a millstone for her, too.

When the final confident chord of Mother's "Hark the Herald Angels Sing" faded, along with our singing, the snapping fire was the only sound for a long moment.

It didn't take long to open our presents. Pat and I each received a practical, wearable gift and one game, book, record, or other item chosen earlier from the Sears catalog. My carefully wrapped gift from Ruthie was Heaven Scent cologne in an angel-shaped bottle. I saved the best for last. Pat's godparents, childless Fred and Sara Branch, were generous to both of us. This year they gave me a cashmere sweater!

Unable to wait two whole days, I opened the little store-wrapped birthday package from them too—a sterling silver spoon pin with a Dutch boy and girl kissing atop the handle. ("Aunt" Sara had seen me as a Dutch girl in a tap number a couple of years ago.) It was a beautiful gift, but it awakened memories of my Cécile spoon and of Yvonne (what was she doing this holy night?), memories that sent me from the room "to try on my sweater" and to hide my misty eyes.

In my bedroom, I pulled on the sweater, added the shiny pin, and turned, freeing hair from collar, to admire the effect. My flushed face stared back at me, betraying the truth within: this picture needed Glenn standing behind me, his hands on my shoulders, his approving grin making my pleasure complete.

My arms crossed to opposite shoulders in a tight hug, my mouth pressed against one hand. Pride was a cold substitute, I thought, for his voice, his scent, his touch.

⌐ ⌐

We drove to Howard Lake for our holiday with the Smith family the day after Christmas. Aunt Mary and Uncle Charlie had moved into a comfortable new rambler with indoor plumbing and modern appliances, built on their land. Just fifty yards away, the little farmhouse that held tender memories for me was rented now. My grandparents' house a few miles away in the small town had been sold. Granddad lived in the new house too, still a jovial presence when he wasn't downstairs puttering with a carpentry project.

My three Smith cousins shared this day. We all missed Uncle

Alvin's family; they had moved to Spokane, Washington. My sense of them now was only what could be gleaned through routine news in Aunt Nettie's letters.

Here among my country relatives, I still felt the uncritical acceptance that flows from caring people who can stand back and watch you grow, unencumbered by all the messy decisions about your upbringing or the consequences of those choices.

When Uncle Charlie teased me about my "boyfriend," Aunt Mary sensed my discomfort, so she took me aside to ask, "And how is Glenn?"

I told her my sad story and added, "Mother thinks I'm stupid."

"And how do you feel about it?" she prodded gently.

"I don't know anymore," I confessed.

"Well, we're never too young to learn," she said, "and never too old to change. Just keep an open heart, and you'll know what's right for you."

My first formal gown, bright blue and strapless, lay on my bed. I pulled nylon stockings up over my legs, carefully straightening the seams all the way up the back.

Do girls, when they are sixteen, have any concept of the power they wield, with shiny hair touching creamy shoulders? Their fresh innocence is like a powder keg waiting for a fuse; it's the stuff that honorable men are willing to fight and die for. Yet the eyes in my mirror focused only on the zit that was threatening to erupt on my jaw. If I had even imagined I'd be going to the Sno Ball, I thought, I wouldn't have eaten all those holiday sweets.

On the morning of my birthday, sixteen long-stemmed roses had been delivered to me. The note, in Glenn's casual handwriting, said simply "Happy Birthday. I miss you."

I went for a long walk before I called him, wanting to be certain I was responding to my own change of heart and not the roses, or even his wishes. Then I waited until Mother left the house. By the time I called to thank him for the flowers, I knew I wanted to see him, even before he asked.

That afternoon, over 7UP and french fries, we agreed that he'd been a creep to give in to a challenge from the guys to stand me up. We also agreed that I was a drip to make a federal case out of it. And finally the breezy banter gave way to real communication and deeper revelations for both of us. I learned that an eighteen-year-old man feels compelled to pass many tests—even against his own nature. It is the cost of fraternizing. And I believe he learned that the tests could have a cost. I know he saw a sixteen-year-old girl too vulnerable to withstand the fallout.

Talking to him, exchanging ideas and feelings, I saw more clearly what had hindered a smooth transition for me and my parents; I saw that adoption should be the beginning of a process, not the end. It should initiate a course of becoming acquainted, sharing, pleasing each other—just as Glenn and I were doing now—not the awful silence that kept the early me a total stranger to my family.

Six days later, I stepped into my blue taffeta gown and zipped it up the back. On my dresser, a flowered china dish, my legacy from Gram Scott, held dried rose petals. From a velvet box I took the rhinestone necklace and earrings Glenn gave me—a belated Christmas gift. He had put the jewelry on lay-by at the wholesaler where he worked, just before we broke up.

Later, when Glenn pinned a white orchid to the cuff of my bodice, he said, ''My girl will be the prettiest girl at the dance.'' I liked the generous compliment and the message his eyes sent—and even the sound of the possessive pronoun.

chapter

twelve

Myths and Realities

In the 1940s, Hollywood produced many memorable classic films like *Casablanca*, *Mrs. Miniver*, and *The Best Years of Our Lives*, but the movie screens were dominated by war stories, B westerns, and predictable musical comedies ("We can save Pop's diner by putting on a show in the old barn").

Continuing episodes of Tom Mix and Hopalong Cassidy serials drew crowds of kids to ten-cent matinees on Saturdays. Adults were lured by Tuesday "bank night" ("Your ticket stub might be drawn for cash!") and Wednesday "dish night" ("This week each and every customer receives a cereal bowl in the lovely Starlight pattern").

Family crisis tearjerkers were surefire favorites. The adoption-myth movies, as I thought of them, were as corny as the other formulas: In a spacious home we see Kathryn, a serious Jennifer Jones type, trying on her white dress for next week's graduation. She decides to borrow her mother's cameo necklace. Opening a box in Mom's dresser drawer, she finds (ta-dum!) her own adoption papers. Kathy tearfully confronts her stunned parents.

129

"How could you lie to me all these years?"

Her mother (Myrna Loy/Irene Dunne) begs her, "Please understand, Kathryn darling, we thought we were protecting you."

After the black and white screen images perform their ritual dance of anguish, Kathy rushes from the house to find her boyfriend, usually named Eddie. They hold hands in a white latticed gazebo in the park while she sobs, "My whole life is a lie. I'm a freak!"

He reassures her, "You're not a freak, you're beautiful. And you should be grateful for the super home you have. I think your folks are swell!"

Now it was Eddie's turn to catch it. "You don't understand—any of you—what it's like not to belong to anyone. Go away. I never want to see you again!"

Gramps knows where to find Kathy; he brought her there once when she was five. In the gazebo, now moonlit, he dries her tears. "The day they brought you home, a perfect little pink bundle, was the happiest day of my life, except for the day I married your grandma, rest her soul."

Kathy shivers in the white graduation dress that nips in at her twenty-two-inch waist. Gramps removes his sweater with the shawl collar and wooden buttons and wraps it around her. He pulls the bill of his wool cap down to the top of his wire-rimmed glasses and walks her home, his thumbs hooked into his suspenders.

Kathy mopes around for a few days while everyone kisses up to her and Dad calls her Princess a lot; it's just long enough to show us how spoiled and ungrateful she is. Then she meets her perky friend Ginger/Babs/Bunny at the soda fountain and spouts some oversimplified clichés: "I realize now that my real parents are the ones who raised me—who fed and sheltered me, sat up all night when I was sick." Her loyalty is touching, but her logic would apply if she'd been raised by a pack of wolves. (That might have made a better movie.)

In the final scene, Kathy, capped and gowned, delivers the valedictory. At the podium she crumples her speech, "The Need for Higher Education in a Changing World," and ad-libs a moving tribute to parental sacrifice while Mom weeps in the front row. We can see that Kathy has put the incident behind her; it's a relief to know she'll never feel curious or troubled again.

When Kathy leads her class to pick up their diplomas, her entire family rises to applaud. Out of nowhere, an orchestra plays appropriate music. (The last theme song I remember was titled "Our Very Own.")

It amused me to imagine pampered Kathryn in some of my situations but, long ago, I had put aside regrets about material or transitory losses. If I missed having pictures of myself before age seven, there were plenty of people who had gaps in their photo albums then; during the Depression, they couldn't afford film for their Kodak Brownie box cameras. In the midst of mourning my lost name, I had read about foreigners arriving at Ellis Island, where impatient immigration officers turned Max Brznitski into Max Cohen for no better reason than to speed up the line. There are many different kinds of survivors.

But I raged within at films that portrayed an adoptee's natural curiosity as disloyalty. The deep need of some adopted people to reconnect, or to learn about their origins, often eluded filmmakers and others who could take their own unbroken history for granted.

Therapy was rare then, even for adults. It was a last resort for disabling mental or emotional problems. For children, at least in my family's circles, counseling was unheard of. The attitude, as I perceived it, toward abused or alienated children who were "lucky" enough to be adopted was this: if your rescuers drop you halfway down the mountain, you should be grateful they didn't just leave you up there.

The adoption films, reflecting the times, didn't suggest intervention for the confused teenager either; rather it was implied that the situation could be dealt with by the family alone. (Of course, the adoptors in the film were uncommonly stable and wise.)

And how my spirit suffered from the movie's simplistic message: if only Kathryn would bury her past, smother her curiosity, and accept her parents' needs as her own, she could fit in perfectly!

But if she obediently stifles her own feelings, Kathryn gains no insights or understanding from her emotional experience. No cure for the secrecy that harmed her. No guidance for those who are entrusted with her physical and emotional health. I believe most adoptions, even infant ones, leave deeply buried questions waiting for permission to be asked and desperately needing open, honest answers.

I knew that for me, the secrecy and capitulation were carrying too high a price, yet I was unwillingly paying it. "Sweet sixteen" and trailing old unspoken hurts behind me like the remains of a child's raggedy blanket. As I finished my junior year, I felt the magical, mystical experience called a happy childhood slipping from my grasp.

I wanted desperately to ensure a happy adulthood, but I didn't know how to go about it. My father didn't look at my needs (he had taught me how to change a tire, but not how to drive). And I couldn't imagine that someone so uninterested in the hurts of my childhood could care about my fears of adulthood.

Patrick was concentrating hard on his own goals. He probably asked about mine, but in a casual way I don't recall. I suspect that Mother's easier way with me could be traced in part to Pat's efforts. If so, he never claimed the credit.

Mother encouraged my independence and clearly expected me to take the initiative in preparing for my future. She was beginning to plan her own. Some months later she would resume her career, a brave move after twenty-five years of managing a home, a move that would prove both exhausting and exhilarating for her. I would watch then, amazed to see her unfold like a flower brought from dim light into full sun, exposing a vibrant and complex center. For now, she was like a graceful bud, partly unwrapped, full of promise.

Early on, I had developed the habit of making it through one phase at a time. Now I had to plan ahead, and it terrified me. I had bouts of confusion and panic, sharper and stronger than I'd ever known. I was a ship with no rudder or anchor, listing helplessly out of control.

What could I do? Nudge reluctant adults to some concern for my future? Rely on Glenn's love to magnify whatever strength and courage I had? A little of each, perhaps, but there was this nagging feeling still that I must claim the best remnants from each of my past experiences and stitch them together into a new quilt of comfort and hope.

Where does one begin? In the center? At the edges? If only I could be shown the first step.

~ ~

Glenn and I had dated for more than a year, enjoying the best that all four seasons had to offer. We explored corners of our diverse Twin Cities neither of us had seen before. Minneapolis and St. Paul, roughly divided by the blue Mississippi, which coils between them, offered a wealth of sights for our eager eyes. We guided a rented canoe over sparkling lakes and spread a picnic on the shore (this was a way I could treat).

He saved to take me to Dayton's Skyroom for lunch, but I insisted on going instead to the mysterious wood-paneled Oak Grill, which adjoined it. I wanted to learn what strange secrets they were guarding in this place that banned "unescorted" women. All I could see was a higher concentration of pipe and cigar smoke. And the Oak Grill was darker, without the Skyroom's stunning view. The men could have it, I thought. And they did—for another twenty years. Then one day, two young women simply walked in and sat down, and after a brief delay their orders were taken. Dayton's management was savvy and principled enough to accept the inevitable graciously.

Glenn satisfied his own curiosity by lunching with me at The Leaves, a downtown café, a windowless molded cave. In its candlelit damp coolness, girls loved to giggle over their tea-leaf fortunes, told so convincingly by a dark woman wearing a gauzy veil and clanky bracelets.

We danced, and listened, to the big bands that appeared at the Prom Ballroom in St. Paul, swaying to Tommy Dorsey's slow ballads and catching the excitement of his incomparable swing numbers. We learned, by watching experts, to do a passable lindy hop. The dance, named twenty years earlier by musician Shorty Snowden in honor of Charles Lindbergh's hop over the Atlantic, had only recently swept the country.

Fine local talent played at the Marigold in downtown Minneapolis and Danceland on Lake Minnetonka. Glenn's Uncle Harry played bass with both local and big touring bands. He would introduce us to band members and buy Cokes for us during intermission.

Uncle Harry was the youngest of Glenn's dad's eight siblings, just ten years older than Glenn and as irreverent and scandalous as the other siblings were conventional. Glenn had eagerly adopted Harry's personality and generosity, yet wisely rejected his young uncle's morals. Uncle Harry would hire us to wax his car if he knew we wanted money for the State Fair (indulging the common notion that unearned money corrupts kids).

Glenn had had many jobs over the past six years, first riding a streetcar downtown to insert pages in Sunday newspapers from early Saturday evening until about three in the morning. Then the thirteen-year-old, in all weather, rode the streetcar back to a stop six blocks from his house and walked home. He had also dug graves at a cemetery, set pins in a bowling alley, and hoisted barrels of beer up flights of stairs to lodge halls. When he got his driver's license he delivered groceries, then orders for a dental lab. He'd gotten his present job for the jewelry wholesaler when he started business college. It left little money after he paid his tuition and the room and board his parents charged as soon as he was out of high school.

My senior year began, curtailing our time together. Glenn and I were close friends and still-chaste lovers. The self-control was not unusual for dependent teenagers then; irate fathers often chose to banish pregnant daughters from their home rather than endure harsh gossip. The same society that kept mentally disabled people in collective darkness preferred to hide or deny pregnancies outside of marriage.

I knew of girls who had taken five-month vacations to "visit an aunt in Seattle." The bulging girls from the home for unwed mothers who strolled around Windom Park in Glenn's neighborhood were mostly refugees from small towns. Glenn's mother, with her missionary circle, visited "the home" before holidays, bringing fancy nut cups and Bible-verse bookmarks.

"You can't help but feel sorry for them," Glenn's mother told me. "Some are only fourteen years old." But then she added, "I just can't understand why some of them are back for the second or third time."

Maybe, I thought, nut cups are not precisely the help they need.

∼ ∼

Glenn and I became closer, and I became more anxious. Emotional investments had betrayed me too often; I didn't trust them. I feared that this attachment too, might be erased like a sand castle at high tide. I began to test our relationship, to goad him into anger. Only when he retreated from me would I let him back in. I hated myself, and even suspected that this subterfuge was a means to avoid the intimacy I needed so much. But what if he got close enough to see the real me, not this phony persona I'd adopted to fit in?

On a perfect autumn evening, Glenn and I went out for ice cream and a long drive. He turned to me after he parked the car in front of my house. His hand rubbed my neck to focus my attention. He didn't know that the sight of his strong hands on the steering wheel, the feel of his thigh against mine, had already accomplished that. A few passionate minutes later, we caught our breath, my head settled on his shoulder. We were breathing as one, yet I felt strangely distant, even from him. I had a sense of floating downward; I needed strong caring arms to lift me up.

I began to talk about my early experiences, telling him more than anyone else knew: the shame of my birth father's crime, my grief over my natural mother's weakness—a grief I was acknowledging to myself for the first time as I spoke the words. And then I told him about the violations.

When I paused for his reaction, there was silence. I pronounced his name with a question mark, inviting a response.

His voice came out of the shadows. "I'm thinking about what you said."

But in those moments when I mistook his pensive silence for indifference, I felt abandoned, frightened that my brittle pain was of no concern to him. Or worse—was he feeling disgust? Disbelief?

"Are you sorry I told you?" I asked.

"No," he said, almost whispering. "I'm sorry I wasn't there to protect you."

⌒ ⌒

Love. I'd planned just to put my toe in the water, and here I was, plunging over the falls. Exciting, but scary. Was I ready? Would I ever be?

With my graduation on the horizon, Glenn wanted my commitment soon—not a far-fetched idea given the number of engaged girls in my class. He began a four-year electrical apprenticeship with the Great Northern Railroad, a step toward securing our future. To do it, he gave up the job he loved. He enjoyed both selling and jewelry, and his boss and mentor liked and trusted him.

When I saw the intricate maze of wires that hid in the massive belly of a diesel train's engine, I was incredulous that anyone could learn to maintain and repair it. Glenn showed me a steam locomotive he trained on, explaining how its power was generated. When the pressure built up in the huge boiler, it was released with a fierce pop as scalding steam gushed from the relief valves. If a worker was on top of the engine when the warning hiss came, Glenn told me, he would want to move very fast.

He showed me the light towers in the railroad yard where he changed 1,000-watt floodlights from a narrow catwalk perched atop a 100-foot pole. The pole, purposely flexible so it wouldn't snap in the wind, swayed in a dizzying dance under the electrician's weight.

I saw firsthand that a rookie apprentice had to prove himself, absorbing taunts and tricks, some that looked dangerous to me. And I had no doubt that the trials were more severe if the greenhorn's dad (and his girlfriend's dad) were company foremen. Glenn took the prods and pranks in stride. "It goes with the territory," he told me. In fact, he said he valued the camaraderie of his fellow railroaders—men he found to be decent and honorable.

I kept putting off promises and intimacy, trying to find breathing space, needing to feel whole before I let go of any part of me.

Mother invited Glenn for Thanksgiving without asking me. I uninvited him, soothing his feelings with a promise of quiet sharing, maybe even planning, for the two of us Friday evening if I could first have some time alone.

I moved through Thanksgiving Day—preparation, dinner, cleanup—quiet and distracted, my thoughts veering deep into neglected places. The few times my attention surfaced, I was surprised how dull our celebration seemed this year. Dad's voice droned on with familiar stories and opinions. Mother was absorbed in the mechanics of providing more steamy-hot dressing and gravy. She was new to these Thanksgiving duties, having inherited them after her mother died. Pat pushed aside his half-eaten pie, announced he'd be home late, grabbed his coat, and left on foot for the home of a friend who would drive to their undisclosed destination.

Glenn called to say good night. "How was your Thanksgiving?" I was grateful he didn't sound hurt or angry.

"Okay . . . and yours?" I asked.

"Oh, I'll start giving thanks tomorrow when I see you." He did sound impatient. "There are so many things I want to talk to you about. Are you sure I can't pick you up at noon?"

"My folks are going car shopping. I could use a few hours by myself."

His pause told me he didn't understand. "Hmm . . . but after seven you're all mine?"

"All yours!"

"I like the sound of that. Sweet dreams." The warm quality of his voice and the content of his words tingled my spine.

⋍ ⋍

I don't remember why I climbed the stairs to Pat's empty bedroom that Friday following Thanksgiving. But once I was there, I moved quickly to the cramped space beneath the eaves that was home to my childhood doll, the doll who had kept, through it all, the name of the child star she resembled. Taking Jane carefully from her box, I held her on my lap. She gazed solemnly back at me, blue eyes unblinking. How I wished she could talk, give me all the answers.

Here I was, balanced on the slippery slope to womanhood. I would be seventeen in just one month. Soon my life would be shaped more by my own actions and desires. Why did I feel so disconnected, incomplete somehow, sitting here with Patty's doll . . . Patty's doll? My heart jumped, my breath caught in my throat. In the attic's chill I felt clammy and weak. How long had I been thinking of Patty in the third person, totally separate from Donna? A very long time? Since that February day when they divided us, convinced me she was inferior, forgettable? "Damn them!" I screamed to the empty house.

Or did I leave her myself, floating away from the pain that terrible birthday night? No, I couldn't excuse them, deny my anger. They were wrong. Not evil, just wrong!

A transplanted child, especially an older one already damaged by circumstances, shouldn't be met with abrupt changes and closed subjects, her responses censored, her history obliterated. The turmoil that lay always within me was not, I decided, all caused by my shameful secret past or shortcomings of my early upbringing.

I wanted Patty back, tried desperately, eyes squeezed shut, to pull her into my present, to unite my broken life and spirit. It was like trying to hold on to a sunbeam.

Inner voices warned me:

"Don't go back. You might not be strong enough this time!"

"You have to distance yourself from the pain."

"You can't be part of both worlds."

No! That was their protective myth, not the truth. I was more afraid of this separateness—unnatural, forced on me. I was shaking, and mildly surprised that Jane's face remained calm.

The Patty part of me, banished from the house like Sis's imaginary friend Eve, had become my scapegoat, the excuse for every defect in me. Claiming Patty meant I would own those faults again.

Or maybe we would own them together, along with some qualities long neglected, held close in my severed child self: curiosity, risk, impulsiveness.

New voices joined in:

"Don't let anyone else define who you are."

"You're never too old to take chances."

"I'm sorry I wasn't there to protect you."

I inhaled deeply. For a moment, I felt wholeness, the Holy Spirit doing her work, the connectedness you feel when you hold a baby close, or stand as a group for the Hallelujah Chorus during Handel's *Messiah*. In that moment, a single thought flooded over me: both of my identities shared one authentic and everlasting spirit!

Here was the continuous thread to hold the quilt of my life together, strong enough to make wrapped saplings as sturdy as a solid tree. Had it also been secure enough, back then, to hold a child in gentle suspension, out of harm's way?

By the time I rose, on legs stiff with cold and tension, doubts and fears were already creeping back, the sense of wholeness escaping like air from a punctured balloon. I had a feeling this reunion, this closure I longed for, would not happen quickly or easily.

I would have to move gently into my parents' denial, open the locked lid carefully. If I told them I needed to reconnect my past before I could plan a future, would they acknowledge and affirm my longing to be accepted as Patty too, or would they cut me adrift emotionally? It seemed important for me to remember I could probably survive if they did. I had survived such things before.

It was growing dark. I heard the kitchen door close, heard voices. I was ready to go downstairs now, and Jane was going with me.

I moved slowly down the steep wooden stairs, my doll facing outward from the crook of my arm, the way nurses display newborns in a nursery window.

I sensed inside me a new beginning.

chapter thirteen

Milestones

A nurse came through the door of my hospital room, a bundled infant cradled in her arm. Like Jane and me, I thought. But this young woman was smiling broadly, her cap cocked forward to accommodate a bristle of ponytail. A cloth diaper for my shoulder swung from her hand. In her, I saw all that I had lacked that momentous day when I climbed down from the attic: humor, confidence, preparedness.

She laid the baby in my outstretched arms. I stroked his fine hair, like silk, and looked into dark blue eyes like mine. Feelings of warmth and wonder engulfed me. For the first time in more than a decade, I was touching my own flesh and blood!

I kissed the red mark on his forehead. One eye was partly closed, giving him a pugilistic look.

"Just a souvenir from the forceps," the nurse assured me. "He'll be perfect by the time he goes home. Stubborn little guy, though— tried to set a record for resisting delivery."

"He's perfect now," I said, cuddling him closer, "and I like my men determined.'' But she didn't need to remind me about the long delivery; the ordeal still owned my memory. ''Where is my husband?'' I asked.

''Home to shave and change his shoes.''

''His shoes?''

''I expect he wore the other ones out, pacing all day and night in the father's room.'' Fathers were not yet allowed in the hospital labor or delivery rooms.

She assured me he'd be back in time for visiting hours, those brief, rigidly enforced periods after lunch and dinner. The babies would be whisked from our rooms before any visitors, even fathers, arrived.

The nurse made sure I had read up on lactation, then hustled toward the door.

I called to her anxiously, ''But when can this boy's daddy see him?''

''Are you kidding?'' she said, chuckling. ''He stood at that nursery window for an hour, waving and laughing at the little guy. I swear, we wondered which one was the baby!''

I was grateful for the glimpse of that precious scene, but I thought I'd explode with frustration at rules that kept us from experiencing, together, these first moments with our son.

I did vaguely remember the recovery room, Glenn's face bending to mine, his hands brushing wet hair off my forehead, and his soothing words: ''Our little boy is perfect. They said you were great. I have to leave for a while.''

I looked at my child's tiny wrist, soft and supple as bread dough. The blue and white beads around it spelled out the name I'd written over and over these past months. Like his Uncle Pat, he would have his mother's maiden name; his middle name would be new, and all his own: Scott Randal. The magnitude of this new responsibility would register later. All I knew at that moment was that I wanted for him to always, always be certain of our love.

Later there would be a little girl, lively and pink, my blood coursing through her veins, too. Her name, Wendy Jill, was inspired by her five-year-old brother's earnest suggestions. I wanted her always to feel loved and secure too, and I hoped she would be curious and humorous and find early the confidence I still struggled to attain.

By the time Wendy was born, Glenn was allowed in my hospital room, masked and gowned, to hold her—precious minutes of bonding. Some years later, a few enlightened hospitals began to allow, then encourage, delivery-helper dads, and we would be envious, listening to their potent, poetic descriptions of shared elation.

But now I reluctantly surrendered my sleepy son to the nurse just as the phone rang.

"Sweetheart!" Mother's voice was joyful. "Were you resting? I can't wait to see you and Scott. Glenn says he's beautiful!" She generously offered to delay her visit to her first grandchild until the second half of the arbitrary visiting hours, to give Glenn and me an hour alone, our first since I'd been wheeled into the labor room.

Dad, I knew, wouldn't come. Walking was too difficult for him now to be wasted on these long corridors. I thought of him as I dozed off and on, first lulled by exhaustion, then alerted by voices and wheels in the hallway. I wondered if he would ever comprehend what I tried to tell him that day so many months before, after my epiphany in the attic.

"Oh, there you are, Snooks," he'd said, hearing the door at the bottom of the stairs close behind me. He turned and saw Jane just as I stepped from the dining room into the brighter light near his chair. Shock registered on his face but, without a word, he picked up his car brochures and began to study them carefully.

"Dad, can I talk to you?" My legs felt weak.

He hesitated. I wondered if he had feared there would be questions one day.

"What about?" he asked, not looking up.

"I need to talk about—you know—before I came here—my other family."

"Nothing to talk about. And you're too old for dolls now. You can put that thing away." His jaw was tight.

"Can you understand that I can't just forget about them? What if someone told you that you could never mention Gram, or your brother William, or anyone you've lost?"

"That's different!" he shouted. He picked up his cane and pointed it at me. I thought he would strike me, although he never had before.

"Those people walked away from you. Your no-good old man

walked away and never looked back!'' (Just whose father was he so angry with, I wondered. Mine? Or his?)

"If it wasn't for me," his tirade continued, "you'd still be in that orphan's home."

I backed away from him, aghast. Mother, shocked into silence too, had come in from the kitchen and stood behind me, pan in hand.

"Lee! Stop it—stop! Why are you saying—?" I turned and she saw Jane. "Oh, God, is this all because of that old doll?" she asked.

"No, Mother," I said. I felt as though my voice came from somewhere else. "It's because of a little girl who *wouldn't die.*"

Dad threw down his cane and picked up his brochures to signal the closing of this subject. Still, something had happened here. I had always been afraid to oppose Dad (could it be because, after my refusal to talk to Daddy in his holding cell, I never saw him again?).

But now I'd faced his wrath—and survived. I understood now why people climb mountains and jump from airplanes: to confront their worst fear in order to conquer it.

I felt sad for my father, this hardworking, honest man who could have given lessons in endurance to a Stoic. He must have dreamed dreams when he left home and school in his early teens to forge a life independent of his aloof father.

I'd seen a picture of Dad and a friend, young men in rakishly tilted derby hats and cocky smiles, looking like Butch Cassidy and the Sundance Kid. A recent photograph of Dad in his Knights Templar uniform, sword drawn, betrayed a trace of that same boyish smile.

Just when did the vision surrender to myopia, hobbling him more even than his worn hip? Had his castles crumbled in the Depression too?

I'd read a story about a man, blind since birth, whose sight was restored. The blessing turned to agony for him because all that he had previously learned and believed was challenged. His touch and taste had painted false pictures. He'd had no perception before of depth and space, and so now he fell and bumped into things more than when he couldn't see. Even though he was thrilled by the colors, he couldn't bear the conflict, and so he simply closed his eyes and refused to see.

While these thoughts raced through my own overloaded senses, I laid Jane on my bed and covered her with a shawl as if she were cold from the attic, as I was. Then I dressed hurriedly for my date with Glenn.

Mother kept coming to my bedroom. "He doesn't mean it," she whispered. "He just doesn't want you remembering sad times."

"No," I told her, "he's afraid I'll have feelings for someone who didn't get stuck supporting me."

She sighed and left. In a few minutes she was back. "We can talk about it when you get home. He'll be at work then."

"Mother," I forced a gentler tone, "don't worry about me. I've been waiting nearly ten years to talk about this. I can wait a little longer." It was almost 7:00. I kissed her, pulled up my coat collar, and left to wait for Glenn on the steps.

☞   ☜

Glenn wasn't surprised to find me outside. I'd waited there before, if Dad was sleeping, so Glenn wouldn't ring the doorbell.

"What are you wearing?" he asked.

"My cashmere sweater. And the locket you gave me. Why?"

"We're going to Jax," he said, hugging me.

The restaurant was popular with the social set and an after-prom treat for young people. Even their special petite filet mignon was $2.25; our dinners, with dessert and tip, would cost a day of apprentice pay.

"What's the occasion?" I asked.

"I'm giving thanks, remember? Let's go. We'll lose our window table if we're not there by 7:30."

Glenn asked them to seat me while he took our coats to the checkroom. Through the window beside me, I watched lazy white flakes just beginning their descent through the heavy air, and I felt as if I were decompressing after a long, dangerous dive, but one where I'd seen the murky water become clearer, infused with light and air. Glenn returned, telling me he had ordered fruit cocktail for both of us. Mine arrived, in its pedestal dish, and beside it on the lacy doily was a small blue velvet ring box.

"What did, uh, when—?" I sputtered.

"I was going to wait until Christmas," he explained, "but when I picked it up today, I just couldn't put it away. It felt like trying to stuff all my hopes and dreams away in a dark drawer.''

I laughed. More of the day's tension drained away. ''I think I understand the feeling!''

The diamond ring he slipped on my finger was lovely, dainty, and a perfect fit. Weeks ago, when he still worked at the jewelers, we had stopped by their showroom one day and he explained different gems and carat weights and casually demonstrated how they sized rings.

Our meal was probably excellent, and no doubt the restaurant's touted service was fine too, but of that night I remember only his eyes, my tears, his voice, my ''yes,'' our hands wrapped together at the table.

It was difficult to linger long in the crowded restaurant; we hadn't learned to like coffee, and the bar was off-limits to underage people.

But the spacious golf chalet that Luanne's father managed, which housed their family apartment along one end, had a fireside lounge in the center, facing the golf course. Any day now, the silent slopes beyond the smooth greens would be dotted with impatient skiers trying to push their heavy wooden skis through a few inches of damp snow.

But when we arrived that evening, a dozen bundled children, cocoa-warmed after their hayride, were just trooping out. The clubhouse attendant knew me well; he wouldn't chase us out until the kitchen was clean and he was ready to lock the doors.

We watched the fire die down, my head on Glenn's shoulder, and I described for him, with a calm that surprised me, my emotional day. My secret glances at our reflection in the wide windows assured me that he was listening carefully.

Finally he said, ''It sounds like your father is really scared.''

''My father—afraid?'' I asked, incredulous at the thought. ''What on earth could he be afraid of?''

''Well, I think that, for once, I understand his feelings.''

''What do you mean?'' I turned to stare at him.

''He's afraid,'' he said gently, ''of losing you.''

I buried my face in his neck, feeling confused by his message but empowered by his warmth and love. The slight lingering scent of his aftershave lotion, the rough tweed of his sport jacket against my cheek, conquered the last bit of my caution. And suddenly, there it was—the delightful response I'd been choking back, protecting myself from. At last it won out, overwhelmed me, and made me laugh and cry all at once. A new desire (or had it grown quietly for a long time?) brushed all others aside: I wanted, more than anything, for him to be as happy as he made me.

And I believed a life that had brought me to this time and place must have been well-guided after all.

꡶ ꡷

Mother and I never actually had the candid talk she hinted at the night of my engagement. She was so buoyed up about the ring, I found myself reluctant to force open old scars now that I'd be moving out in a matter of months. It was enough that she answered the few questions I put to her.

"My sister Yvonne promised to write to me. Do you have any idea why she didn't?"

"Well, one letter did come. We sent it back. Dad—we—thought it would be best for you, to cut all ties. I'm sorry if this upsets you."

"I'm glad you told me," I sighed, picturing Yvonne's child face, hurt and bewildered.

"But," her words rushed out, "I drove down to see her, tried to explain. Well, you had just stopped sleepwalking, bed-wetting, and we wanted you to forget." Seeing my tears, she added softly, "I brought her a present, a furry toy kitten. She was so excited over it."

My emotions seesawed from numbing depths to giddy heights. Yes, I thought, that sounds like my sister.

Another time, Mother broached the subject herself:

"I want you to know we never wanted the sweet child we found to *die*." Obviously, my remark about the girl who wouldn't die had disturbed her greatly.

"Well," my defenses rose, "you didn't always seem to want her here!"

"How can I explain?" She sat down and studied her hands, upturned in her lap. "I wanted to go back and do it over—wanted you to be born again—all mine." She looked at me intently while she searched for words.

"Maybe I was jealous of the ties you had." She came to me and took my face in her hands. Her lashes were wet, her eyes full. ''And you thought I was rejecting *you* along with those ties.

''Oh, Donna dear,'' she said, now using the shorter name I preferred, ''of course—how would a child know the difference.'' She said it sadly, not even as a question. If there were more words in her mind, they caught in her throat while she held me tight.

I felt our souls touch in the mercy and truth of that moment. With relief, I sensed that shattering the silence had liberated her emotions as much as mine.

chapter fourteen

A Time to Weep

It was an autumn like no other, in that eighteenth year since my marriage. The trees, under dull gray skies, had surrendered their leaves early, before their blazing colors peaked. At the same time, the long hopeful days of summer deserted us, leaving harsh, bitter reality.

My brother arrived for the second time, from his home in California, to assess Mother's condition and decided again that she would recover fully. It was easy for Patrick to believe something he wanted so desperately.

My own denial had been assaulted with hard evidence—her rapidly failing memory, drooping eyes—over the last alarming few weeks, and I feared the worst even before the diagnosis finally came.

Mother was more alert, but so sad, when I went to her hospital room the afternoon before her surgery. She sat up in bed, hair combed, eyeglasses in place. I tried to guess her state of mind, hoping to reassure her despite my own leaden fear. But she wanted to talk about me—about my childhood, of all things.

"I saw your strength as defiance at the world. It was as if you needed no one. It frightened me. I didn't know then that it was courage."

"Nothing so noble, Mother. Just the armor that got me through the strife." But her candid words, spoken with such effort, washed over me like a benediction, with power to cleanse and heal.

She wondered aloud why I hadn't been given more: "You were such a wonderful, undemanding child." She tilted her head back to look straight at me through the lower band of her glasses—a gesture, I knew now, that could be a symptom of a brain tumor. Wearily, she said, "I don't understand why you never had a bicycle."

While the full impact of her words hit me, her eyes turned toward the window, and she blinked from even that moderate light. She didn't see the tears that streamed down my cheeks and hung from my chin.

"It's all right, Mother," I said hoarsely. "I probably never asked for one." I went to sit beside her, thanking God for this woman who had been so loving and supportive to my family over the past eighteen years, a woman who continued to blossom and grow, even while she helped me do the same. Touching her cheek, I said, "For you to worry about me, at a time like this, makes me feel very loved."

The next day, after her surgery, her speech was gone. For the next couple of months we were limited to what Patrick's wife, Nancy, called having conversations with our eyes. I was grateful that she had said aloud, when she still could, how much she valued me.

⌒ ⌒

Two days after Mother died, I leafed grimly through the newspaper, needing to check the accuracy of her obituary. A poem caught my eye, simply because the author's last name was the same as that of the funeral director's assistant who had met the day before with Dad, Pat, and me. Afterward, with Mother's pastor, we had talked about her favorite Bible verse ("Whatsoever things are lovely, think on these things") and her favorite hymn ("Just for Today"). We also adopted Nancy's suggestion for a memorial—an annual Laura Scott Christian Nursing Award at St. Mary's Hospital.

I read the poem slowly:

A Farewell
By Charles Kingsley

My fairest child, I have no song to give you,
No lark could pipe to skies so dull and gray.
But, ere I leave, one message I must give you,
Just for today.

Be good, sweet maid, and let who will be clever;
Do noble things, not dream them, all day long;
And so make life, death, and that vast forever,
One grand sweet song.

It was as though my mother had found a way to share her music with me, her poetry-loving daughter.

Our plane took off for Phoenix on time. I held Glenn's hand, grateful that he'd suggested a warm March respite for us. My husband, who had returned to a sales occupation against dire warnings from both our fathers, believed strongly in the therapeutic value of travel. It had been a cold, weary four months since Mother died, just three days before Thanksgiving. While she was ill, I had quit a job that wouldn't grant me time off, and this winter even the freelance writing I enjoyed had gone sour.

Mother's death had hurt Glenn deeply too. Her acceptance of him had been offered as a gift from the beginning, without controls or conditions. He repaid this blessing by treating her with indulgent good humor. Sometimes it annoyed me that they exempted each other from criticism, but I knew it made my life easier to have the two adults closest to me be so fond of each other.

For now, we wanted to focus on planning a celebration for Scott's graduation. We knew our preoccupation with Mother's illness and death had put his important senior year of high school in the background. And Dad, lonely and needful, had been leaning heavily on us too. Glenn had characterized Dad's words after the funeral as the saddest he'd ever heard. "I never knew how much I loved her," Dad had said, "until she was gone."

As soon as we broke through the pillows of clouds, I felt an unworldly peace, a sense of flying alone, apart from the aeronautical science that held me, detached even from the warm hand in mine.

There atop the unbroken puffs of pure white, I knew at once that Mother was near, she was at peace, telling me to grow on.

My turn, now, to try to perfect that imperfectable gift called love.

                          *   *

Dad's death was sudden, from a stroke, five years after Mother's malignant brain tumor claimed her life at age sixty-eight.

For several years Dad had spent winters in California, renting a small apartment a short drive from Patrick's house. When Dad's life ended there in February, Patrick and his wife flew to Minneapolis on the airplane bearing Dad's body while we initiated funeral arrangements.

I discovered that it is a strange passage to bid farewell to the last member of your older generation and suddenly inherit that position yourself. I wondered if new insights or wisdom would be mine as a result.

During the few days Patrick and Nancy stayed with us, we went to the stucco bungalow and sorted through our parents' furniture and forty years of accumulated household goods. Some had now become cherished keepsakes. A few had become, with their owners' deaths, merely superfluous. We divided the things to keep among family members, including Patrick's four children and my two.

Dad's car and all of his personal things—clothing, books, his few pieces of jewelry, even his father's journals—were in California. So, on their next visit, when Nancy handed me a small box, saying, "This was in Dad Scott's things," I expected to find something of his.

Instead I found the award ribbons from my high school all-star field hockey and basketball teams. I was stunned that he had carried them with him.

The box also contained a single snapshot of two little girls.

"That must be you, with one of your little friends," Nancy said. I looked at it with shocked recognition: the picture of Yvonne and me on the morning we were separated. So the state school had sent me a copy, as they'd promised, and my father had kept it from me. But why didn't he destroy it, I wondered, if he didn't want me to see it?

My new senior status in the family had endowed me with neither wisdom nor a complete sense of belonging, and my father's motives would remain a mystery to me.

A few months after Dad died, when I no longer expected to hear his deep voice every time I answered the telephone, I began to think about finding Yvonne.

Who could it hurt now? Pat? My children? With my fortieth birthday behind me, I felt a strong yearning to connect with the beginnings of my life, and I had heard of searches consuming many years. Glenn expressed his misgivings.

"You could get hurt," he said. "I know you still think about Yvonne, but it might be best to keep the memories of her that you have." It was not the encouragement I needed. Still, I made a list of places to start.

From a phone call to Owatonna City Hall, I learned that a fire had burned some records; what remained was with the state welfare people. At the Minnesota Department of Public Welfare in St. Paul my call was answered by Ruth (that name again!) Weidell. She jotted down my information and then searched her files.

"Here it is," she said, returning to the phone. "Every time Yvonne moved, she sent us a letter with her address, just in case you contacted us." The kind voice continued. "She is married and has four children. They live in Minneapolis."

"But why," I asked, incredulous, "didn't you just give her my name?"

"Oh, we couldn't do that because you were adopted, so privacy rules applied. However, because Yvonne stayed at the state school until she was eighteen, with a few stints away to work for families, we are free to tell you about her."

So, after just two phone calls, I stood in my kitchen, holding in trembling hands the address and telephone number of the sister I hadn't seen for a third of a century.

I was still rooted there, minutes later, when Glenn came home. He took the address carefully from my hand and pointed out a fact I'd missed completely: in this city of half a million people, her home was across the alley from the house Scott rented, near St. Mary's Hospital.

Glenn and Wendy encouraged me to call Yvonne that evening; they knew I wouldn't eat or sleep until I did. Wendy, already perceptive at seventeen, suggested I make the call in private, from our bedroom.

A woman answered. To my query she replied, "This is Yvonne." (Was there a trace of a lisp?)

I told her my married name and asked, "Was your name Pearson before you married?"

"Yes," she said carefully.

"Mine was too," I said.

"Patty! Oh! Is this Patty? My God," she yelled to the background voices, "it's Patty!"

"I got your name from state records," I explained, emotion cracking my voice.

"Yes," she said. "I was sure you'd call some day." I could visualize her hand fluttering, her eyes wide.

When our first flush of excitement waned, Yvonne told me she was a licensed practical nurse, training the state provided before she left Owatonna. Her husband was recently disabled by severe diabetes. Although she was diabetic herself, she cared for him and their four children and also took on some home nursing assignments. She spoke tenderly of the elderly woman who was her current patient.

I condensed my life into a few paragraphs for her too.

Then, as we began to arrange for our first meeting, I said, "I'm eager to hear what you remember about our parents and brother, and the orphanage."

Silence. Had I moved too fast, pushed her beyond her comfort zone? She cleared her throat. "There is something you should know," she said gently, her voice quivering. She plunged on. "I have stayed in touch, through the years, with our mother. She lives here in town.''

Her words jolted me as if someone had grabbed me from behind in the dark. Yvonne continued talking—something about our aunts, uncles, and cousins scattered here and there—while I breathed deep to stop trembling.

I managed to tell Yvonne I needed time to digest the news about Momma. She agreed, with no further explanation from me, and invited my family to her home on Saturday, when her children could be there. I believe both of us needed all our energy for our own reunion. Momma would have to wait.

On Saturday, exactly at the appointed time, Glenn stopped the car and nodded toward one of the boxy frame houses nestled close together along the block. ''That's the one.'' The house was almost within field-goal range of Scott's, but he worked Saturdays, so we agreed he should meet my relatives another time.

From the back seat, Wendy asked, ''Are you okay, Mom?'' in the same patient, caring tone she used with the mentally retarded adults she assisted in her summer job.

''Yes, honey, thanks, I'm fine.'' It was true. My feelings about Yvonne were clear-cut and positive. She was an innocent victim whose devotion to me had been dependable, even tenacious. I simply longed to see her face again.

Still, the three of us walked the few feet from the curb to her door feeling awkward. There were no how-to manuals for such an occasion.

As soon as my foot touched the bottom step, my sister opened the door wide. Our embrace only partly absorbed the shock of seeing the nine-year-old of my memory transfigured into a woman of forty-two, shorter now than me, and darker too. My sister's welcoming hug was self-conscious, with her family lined up behind her, waiting to meet me.

Her short-cropped hair was still curly, with some wiry gray strands. Her body was not as thick as I had imagined when she told me on the phone that she had put on ''a lot of weight.'' Her alert blue eyes and earnest manner were just as I remembered; I believed I could have recognized her anywhere on the strength of those two features.

Yvonne's husband, Virgil, was quiet and polite, and their three youngest children—Beth, Dawn, and David—followed his lead. The oldest, Jim, a husky eighteen-year-old, hovered near his mother protectively, alert to every movement. He indicated chairs for us, off to one side, while he and his sisters closed in around their mother on the couch.

Their small dog, indifferent to guard duties, nuzzled my ankles and begged to be petted.

"Patty, come here!" Beth called. Yvonne, embarrassed, rushed to explain. "All my dogs have been named Patty. It was just my way of—well—keeping you closer, I guess." She was clearly uncomfortable.

I laughed, feeling the tension break. "I'm honored," I said. "I love most dogs, and she is a sweet one." Wendy, as always, caught the spirit quickly, telling them, "Then you'll have to name your next one Donna." Laughter and a few chuckles warmed the room; even Jim showed just a flash of a very nice grin.

Wendy talked to the two young girls while Glenn befriended little David, with help from my frisky namesake. Jim kept stretching across the coffee table, silently handing me more photo albums before I could finish the previous ones. I sat in their wooden rocking chair sipping coffee, my shoes flat against the bare floor so my lap could accommodate the growing stack of albums. I could only guess at the identities of most of the subjects.

The pictures captured Yvonne's devotion to her family and good times with other relatives and friends. While I flipped pages, she spoke about her children, their schoolwork and jobs. Her pride in them seemed to add to her sense of self-worth, and I glimpsed the capacity she still had for nurture and sacrifice.

With the preliminaries over, I leaned back and set my coffee mug down. I felt happily expectant, primed for some excitement over our new relationship, but the mood in Yvonne's living room was no more lively than the artificial flowers on the table between us.

Something else was happening here. I forced myself out of my own self-absorbed reverie and tried to consider what Yvonne's family (not to mention my own) might be feeling. Did it feel threatening to suddenly have a stranger own a chunk of her emotions? Were they struggling with some unexpected ambivalence?

Yvonne's restraint could mean she felt torn between expressing sincere feelings for me and reassuring her family of their exclusive claim to her. She might have been walking this tightrope ever since my phone call.

The conversation had turned to sports and weather. At Beth's courteous offer to make more coffee, Glenn sent our secret signal across the room; it was time to go. He was right. I felt suddenly drained, and sure that when my sister and I met again, on more neutral ground, we would both be more comfortable.

Now, sensing this wariness I didn't fully understand, I hesitated to ask Yvonne what she knew of our birth family. It could be awkward for her, and staying longer would test my own family's patience. Yet I couldn't leave without asking. I avoided the other faces and looked directly at my sister. "Can you tell me anything about Daddy, or Duane?" I hadn't meant to sound desperate.

She sighed. "Not very much, but I'll try." She avoided the other eyes too. I sensed that she had not discussed some of this before with her family.

She told me Daddy had written to her several times after I left the orphanage, but she completely lost track of him after our parents were divorced. Momma (Judith, as I referred to her now) had been widowed twice since then and now lived in an apartment less than ten miles from my home.

With each disclosure I felt more vincible, but as Yvonne talked a quiet determination grew in her voice. She stood and moved toward me. Her children turned their knees to clear her path. She paused to take some drawings from the end table, then she pulled a chair up next to me and reached for my hand, seeming either oblivious or defiant of the room's undercurrents. Here was the sister I knew!

It was like watching a plucky cat rescued from the bottom of a well, ready to spring out of the bucket and reclaim her old turf.

Yvonne continued her story slowly: Grandpa died in his nineties, just a few months before, still clinging to the hope of seeing me again. Through a blur of tears, I looked at the pencil sketches that she handed me; Grandpa's drawing style was remarkably like my own.

But it was only when Yvonne told me about Duane that I broke down and wept. Our brother, she'd learned, was a young teenager when he ran away from his adoptive home, and was never found.

Reflecting later on our meeting, I realized that it lacked the exuberant bliss of every reunion I'd witnessed on television. (Maybe those were more complex than they appeared.) But it was enough, for now, to find some closure. The memory of our most recent good-bye—a tight hug and "We'll talk soon"—replaced a thirty-three-year memory of two children wrenched apart on a cold February morning.

Not that the old images departed easily; it took several days to wash them away in floods of tears.

Another reunion loomed ahead. I was grateful that Yvonne was making the arrangements for my meeting with Judith. My feelings about our birth mother were intricate, woven through with questions I was sure I'd never ask her: "Why didn't you fight for us? Yvonne said you married again—?" For years, I hadn't been able to picture her face without Laura's superimposed over it.

Oddly, I had assumed Judith was dead, although she would only be in her mid-sixties. She had seemed so frail, even as a young woman. Or maybe I believed that no woman could survive the loss of her husband and three children.

I decided to meet her alone; it might be easier for her that way. As it happened, I'd recently completed a six-month training course for volunteer crisis counselors. Surely I could draw on those skills.

In the small apartment she'd shared, until recently, with Grandpa, I found her more fragile and dispirited than I remembered. Her own memory seemed to screen out all but the most benign events, while my senses churned with the emotions of our shared history, nearly five of my most formative years. But I did not envy her detachment; somehow I wanted to feel it all keenly.

She asked polite questions of me: ("What are your children's names?") and avoided topics of substance. Yvonne had warned me

Judith wouldn't discuss our early years, or our father, even with her. Still, I asked if she had any photos of my first five years.

"I wouldn't know where to look," she said. "I've moved so many times." Then, changing course, "You still look like my sister Ruth."

"And you resemble Yvonne and her daughter Beth," I told her.

"I took care of Yvonne's children when they were younger so Yvonne could work," she said with a hint of pride. I could imagine that her grandchildren had filled a void in her life.

"I'm glad you had another chance to be a mother to Yvonne."

In a tired voice she replied, "Yes, I was glad she didn't leave too." I was stunned. Did she mean Duane and I had left *her*? She was obviously glad that Yvonne had remained in state custody.

I had no right to judge a woman whose life had been so harsh, but I suspected it was too late for her to mother me. She told me again that Grandpa had never stopped hoping to see me, right up until his death three months ago. It surprised me that, with several siblings, she was the one who had cared for her aged father (or might he have been caring for her?), but I was greatly saddened not to have met this man whose genes might be a source of my strength and optimism.

In time, my response to Judith mellowed into simple kindness: inquiries about her health, an armful of lilacs from my yard, photographs of my family. I was relieved she didn't press for more. I did not step onto the bridge she and Yvonne had built over the swirling waters. It looked just strong enough to hold the two of them.

With Yvonne, I explored the old state school buildings in Owatonna (now the West Hills complex of city services). In the town's library, we were shown a folder of clippings and photographs related to Minnesota's only state school—puny evidence of thousands of children with a unique shared history. I found no books on the topic there, or later in my search of larger state libraries and the Minnesota Historical Society's reference library and archives, only the official superintendent's reports and one probing article.

On other occasions, my sister and I met to exchange memories over iced tea and salad. Her "indenture" experiences were brutal; they haunt her and pain me, but she found relief in exhuming feelings that had been buried alive. Still, our long separation had made real closeness unreachable, artificial. Our cloak of sisterhood had been ripped apart; even though we had not torn it ourselves, it could not be repaired seamlessly. We settle for a friendship with tender undertones; remnants of her protectiveness and my gratitude.

Soon after the reunions, Glenn and I attended the wedding of Yvonne's son Jim, who was about to enter military service. I was excited about seeing Ruth and Willard, the aunt and uncle I remembered, and other relatives I recalled dimly. At the church reception, I could sense their curiosity as clearly as if I were back in the second grade again. The relatives stood in a group, watching me, but there was no Uncle Alvin to pull me across the room, to start the process. My own attempts to extend my hand, start conversations, fell flat and awkward as a hymnal hitting the floor during worship.

The sudden events threw my own family and friends off balance too. Patrick reacted quietly to the exciting news I shared across long-distance phone lines. We had preserved an affectionate relationship despite the miles between us, but he never referred to my discovery again.

Friends with adopted children felt vaguely threatened; searches were uncommon then, all records sealed tight. Others, wanting a storybook ending, were dismayed to learn that my relationship with my natural relatives ranged from casual to distant.

By petitioning the court I was able, because my adoptive parents were dead and Judith gave consent, to recover my early medical and personal records—another victory over ignorance. And now I have an answer when a doctor asks "Do you have a mother or sister who had breast cancer?"

I even obtained my real, honest-to-goodness birth certificate, acknowledging the birth of Patricia Ann Pearson. I kissed the name on the paper, welcoming Patty back to legally sanctioned life. Soon afterward, I needed a passport for my first trip to Europe. I took my authentic new document, my adoption papers, and our marriage certificate to the county office. At last, I could prove the true progression of my identity!

But the clerk would not accept my original birth document be-

cause it bore the stamp "not for official use." I was forced to retrieve my counterfeit birth certificate from the bottom of our safe-
deposit box. The falsified paper was accepted without question.

I had recently organized a team of volunteers from my suburban
church—including Scott, a college student at the time—to tutor
inner-city children with learning disabilities. From my early records I
discovered that, for my six weeks of kindergarten before we were
taken to Owatonna, I attended Madison School, where I now volun-
teered. Our old apartment address was also revealed in the records
now in my possession. The building had been replaced by a storefront
with offices above, but from there I could trace my route to the park,
its paths now navigated by youngsters wearing jazzy shoe skates, and
to the tiny grocery store-turned-coffeehouse.

The discoveries that were amazing and dramatic to me produced a
letdown of major proportions. My bittersweet reunions, far from the
flashbulb scenario, appeared to some to be disloyal and insensitive.
My emotional upheaval was met with near indifference; even my immediate family seemed uncomfortable, uncertain how to respond. It
was an uncharted detour from their Scott-bound genealogy.

I felt more isolated than in the tuberculosis sanitorium. Never a
conformist, I'd found myself holding minority positions from time to
time, but now I felt like the only person who'd ever had this experience. The stress weighed so heavily, I wondered how I could have
been so naive as to plunge in, with no resources (maybe an adoptees
rights organization?) to support me.

I often wished I'd had Mother's help in liberating myself from the
ghosts of my childhood. I was sure she would give it now if she could.

☞ ☜

Without Laura's help, I decided, my lonely odyssey was over; no
more delving into my past. The resolve lasted many months, until it
gave way to an insistent curiosity, like a tongue probing a sore tooth.
Armed with my genuine birth document, which gave my father's
full name, birth date, and occupation, I went to the old Hennepin
County stone courthouse (a building I still avoided when possible),
walked boldly past the Father of Waters statue, and stopped at the
bulletproof glass that shielded the sheriff's reception area. The

woman there sent me back past the statue again and down the hall to the criminal records division. There they found no record whatsoever of his incarceration, but the clerk told me they destroy such records when the subject dies, unless the crime was homicide.

In other government buildings, the county and state death records yielded no death certificate. Had he died in another state? Or was he living, his record expunged because it contained only the one offense?

I questioned Yvonne again. She remembered that Judith did tell her he had married, so any further checking could be more intrusive than I thought.

I asked her for details about Duane's disappearance. She explained that soon after she left Owatonna she was able to learn, from a former staff member there, the name of the Minnesota town where he'd been sent. Because it was a small community, she only had to drop into the small café there a few times and ask casual questions to learn the family's name. The townspeople all knew the boy's history, although he was thirteen by then. She contacted his adoptive parents, but they were unwilling to arrange a meeting with their son—no longer called Duane. They did agree that she could phone them discreetly, at carefully appointed times, to check on his well-being. Nearly two years later, in one such call, she received distressing news: Duane had run away weeks before, leaving no trace.

Because the family didn't sound distraught enough to suit her, Yvonne was skeptical; maybe they just wanted her to leave them alone. Back to the café she went (still my resourceful sister). Unfortunately, the good citizens there verified that the boy had run away, and a couple of them added their own take on it: that the fifteen-year-old was a "whippersnapper," but he "had enough smarts to survive anything."

꒰ ꒱

It was time to decide, once and for all, whether to search for the two men from my distant past. My birth father, now seventy, might have two or three generations of a whole new family. Duane would be forty now, if his survival was as certain as the café patron predicted.

My decision to search for Yvonne had been easy; I was sure she'd want to see me too. Discovering Judith was accidental, but I'd have had no qualms about searching. I don't subscribe to the idea that birth parents are entitled to permanent protection of their identity from their own offspring. How can any parent justify denying the existence of a child? (Sometimes the child's physical health or emotional well-being is at stake.) The most obvious peril for the absent parent, being "found out" by a present-day family, can be avoided by honesty up front (not a bad idea in any case).

Usually there is no conflict, either because the birth parent is willing to be found or because, for whatever reason, the adult child doesn't initiate a search. But if a clash occurs, I believe the child's right to learn about her or his parentage is preeminent.

It is becoming more common for adoptive parents to help their grown child search, an example of unselfish love in action. And then there are open adoptions, which allow the child to be grounded in reality all along.

Siblings are another matter. Reunions with them should be balanced with their own preferences (and, when they are minors, the wishes of their adoptive parents). I admired Yvonne's restraint in not interfering in Duane's adolescent life, although she could easily have contacted him then.

Rights aside, the results of another search could be uncertain, even tragic, and there were other demands on my energy. With our younger child in college, I was enjoying a new job in public relations, serving as president of my church congregation, and lending a hand to a political campaign. Glenn's parents, in failing health now, needed all the attention we could both give them.

I chose not to forge ahead. The decision was not made lightly, but prayerfully. One day, with sensations too broad and deep for tears, I entrusted their memories to a permanent, cherished place in my heart, a letting-go that brought its own quiet peace.

chapter

fifteen

Remembrance

Ever since the day Yvonne and I had driven to Owatonna and found few traces of the children, I had watched for Owatonna stories in my bookstore and in the library's copy of *Books in Print*. In ten years, I found only a single chapter in one book, describing the author's brief stay in cottage five.

I began to research the opening of the state public school, gingerly at first, in a detached way, as if it had nothing to do with me personally. (So why the guilt pangs?)

In the course of that effort, I heard about plans for a reunion of former residents. I went, and listened eagerly to their stories. They were told with good-humored one-upmanship, yet there was always a layer of pain underneath.

A woman told me her treatment at the orphanage was "very good," then later in our conversation said, "You know, we were not allowed to cry. To this day, I cry only when I'm alone, and then I do it silently."

Many men's stories betrayed this dichotomy too. After he described the experience as "not too bad if you played the game their way," one man's eyes misted when he recalled seeing broken bones in hands that had tried to shield a small body from a radiator brush.

Those who remained there until adulthood walked a hard road. One, Jim Razor, told of cruelty at the hands of a few of Owatonna's staff and a sadistic farmer to whom he was indentured. Because Razor, a Native American, had a harsher experience than most, his story was rejected by some former staff members who were present that day, and even by some former wards who preferred to remember their experience dispassionately.

These staff members, who might all have been kind and blameless, insisted that abuse, if any, occurred only as isolated incidents (and certainly "abuse" is defined differently today), but there is no doubt that some cruelty was institutionalized. For example, girls who became pregnant by the fathers or sons in their indenture or foster homes were sent (until 1915) to a reformatory called the State Training School in Red Wing, Minnesota, and after that date to the Minnesota Home School for Girls, a state facility for delinquents in Sauk Centre, Minnesota. Their babies were automatically sent to the Owatonna school's nursery building as second-generation wards of the state. There, the nurses amused themselves by inventing names for them, so that some grew up with names like Napoleon Bonaparte, Florence Nightingale, and Ulysses S. Grant.

Still, for many who left to enter military service or take jobs, leaving the school was like losing a family again. They often wrote "home" to the matrons, to whom some even assigned their GI insurance. Their family trees were not slender ones with branches, but rather a large spruce that had sheltered many pine cones and dropped them all around.

Harvey Ronglien, who stayed until adulthood, still lives in Owatonna and writes occasional poignant columns about his state school days for the *Owatonna People's Press*. Although he puts a generous, positive face on his own experience, he also recalls many former cottagemates who were later incarcerated, shot by police, died of alcoholism or suicide. He writes of others who have kept their state school years a secret, even from their spouses and children. After former ward Napoleon Bonaparte died, his daughter told Ronglien, "He never told us how he got that name." (Records indicate that he was abandoned, nameless, on the steps of the orphanage and entrusted to its nursery staff.)

Even those who, like Ronglien, went on to find love and fulfillment in their lives acknowledge the heavy cost of those loveless years and the resulting struggle for emotional balance.

We who were, at some tender age, grafted onto another family's tree fall prey to a more insidious, isolated feeling. It comes if this defining experience in our lives is never acknowledged. It comes with the burden of gratitude sometimes expected from us, even though natural-born babies are deemed a blessing to their families.

Most of us feel vulnerable, in various ways. Some, like Jim Razor, not knowing when the nightmares will start—or end. Others keeping silence, not sure when the secret will be revealed.

After the reunion, I felt privileged to have heard these voices, usually so silent in the world, shed their inhibitions and undeserved shame to share their stories with others who could understand. I wished they could speak out more freely and claim their rightful, dignified place in history.

Unknown to me then, others were wishing that too.

On July 3, 1993, more than a century after the jubilant opening of the Owatonna State Public School for Dependent and Neglected Children, several hundred people gathered on those same grounds to remember the children who had lived there. This time clouds darkened the sky, there were no bands or flags, and the invited dignitaries had declined to attend. But the people who crowded around the small cemetery were proud of their year-long fund-raising effort. Now the impersonal numbered grave markers were topped with crosses bearing the names of the children who never left.

At the cemetery's entrance, a new arching brick monument was engraved with these words: "May the love you lacked in life be your reward in heaven." In front of the old Romanesque administration building (now serving as Owatonna's City Hall), a bronze statue of a boy and girl awaited its unveiling. A collection of memorabilia from the school's fifty-eight years had found a home in the circular tower room off the building's entry.

Glenn and I stood in line, waiting to examine the photographs, boxing trophies, radiator brushes, and other relics. Two of our granddaughters had come along, bringing a genuine curiosity about my experience there. They were nine and seven years old—the same ages Yvonne and I were when we said good-bye on these steps.

Inside, I stared at a photograph in the glass case: Yvonne and me on the day of our separation. A day full of loss. Loss of sister, friends, school, belongings, name, self. I let myself own the injustice and hurt of that day, no longer needing to depreciate or excuse it. As I conceded the force that day exerted in my past, I felt it being stripped of present power.

Behind me, I could hear hushed comments about various artifacts—a sled, a schoolbook, a pair of worn clunky shoes. A few people were laughing; others sobbed quietly. Turning around, I saw a determination about them too, as they embraced their right to acknowledge profound losses many had tried to ignore for most of a lifetime.

The memorial service was wonderfully touching and appropriate. The bronze statue was well crafted; it portrayed the children's stoic side well, but metal couldn't capture the sparkle in their eyes. I remembered them as resourceful, mischievous, curious, resilient— much like children everywhere, despite their trials.

Looking across the grounds, I could almost see them: resourceful boys making slingshots from old inner tubes and a catcher's chest protector from a gunnysack filled with hay. Mischievous children raiding a farmer's melon patch to supplement their dinner of creamed cod and parsnips. In the building that towered over the monument, I'd known the curious ones who ran away many times because they "wanted to see what's out there." I'd seen resilient girls return from abusive outplacements and assume other tasks— waiting tables and caring for the younger children—with quiet dignity.

The unveiling of the statue was interrupted by a downpour. It came as suddenly as the interruptions, decades earlier, in the child-hoods of Owatonna's "forgotten children," remembered now for posterity.

⌒ ⌒

A couple of weeks later, on a sultry hot night, I sat alone on our small deck, my favorite secluded spot, and watched the sky turn from blue-gray to pink, and then to orange. The familiar scents and tranquil sounds of my refuge, normally soothing, merely contrasted now with my restlessness.

After a while, Glenn found me there. "What's on your mind?" he asked, while his fingers found the tense muscles in my shoulders.

"The Owatonna memorial service," I said, slumping forward, trying to relax.

"I thought you were happy about that."

"Oh, yes, it was comforting to recognize the collective experi-ence of the children, but each one had an individual struggle too. Can any museum or statue convey those as clearly as the oral histories we heard? I've been journalizing again, trying to sort it all out."

"Didn't some people at the service, when they heard that you write, offer their stories to you?"

"Yes," I said, turning to face him, "and don't think I wasn't tempted. But their memories are so precious and personal, and there is still a lot of protective denial, loyalties to guard . . ."

"And I suppose you have some of the same reservations about sharing your own story?" he asked.

My doleful expression gave him the answer.

"Well," he went on, "the truth can sometimes be painful, but wouldn't it tell us something about how these situations affect kids?"

"When did you get so smart?" I asked, taking both his hands.

"You finally noticed!"

We stood close, silent for several minutes. The leaves were rus-tling now in our towering red maple tree, planted as soon as the yard completed its service as a ball field for our children. The breeze held a scent of rain, the promise of relief from the oppressive heat.

"So," Glenn asked me, "how would such a story begin?"

"Hmm, maybe with a little girl who dreamed of a prince."

"Sounds good to me," he said, holding our back door open. "Just answer one important question."

"I'll try," I said, bracing for a tough one.

"This prince guy—did she ever find him?"

Acknowledgments

Minnesota is a great place to write! Academic and professional resources abound, aided by a high regard for books and the cooperative and friendly spirit that writers feed on.

Every librarian, historian, and clerk who assisted my research was capable and courteous beyond my expectations. To my relief, the searches I feared would be tedious were often merely a challenge to them, and I am grateful.

If I needed help with some facet of writing, I could find a class in the University of Minnesota's continuing education program. (By now, I could be their poster woman!) When I needed a week of focused study, I turned to the University's Split Rock Arts Program on the Duluth campus. There, Christina Baldwin taught me to challenge the censor within. Several writers from my 1994 class are still available for wise counsel and a sympathetic ear.

When writing this story became difficult, I could count on encouragement from my writer's group at the Loft, a Twin Cities–based literary arts community. My thanks to all of them, especially

D. Perry Kidder, Kathy Ryan, and Meg Cogelow, because they have been with me from my book's beginning, and that is a lot of angst to share. I hope I am as helpful to them as they are to me.

The Minneapolis Writer's Workshop offers an annual weekend conference with a dozen speakers on various aspects of writing and publishing. I always find a wealth of information there.

With all this home-state help, it feels providential to me that my manuscript found its publisher at home, at the University of Minnesota Press. I am grateful to everyone at the press who has had a part in this book's production, including the director, Lisa Freeman, whom I thank for having confidence in my story. Todd Orjala guided the publication through many stages, always showing respect for my concerns while giving his professional advice. Mary Byers and Becky Manfredini provided expert supervision for editing and production. Copyeditor Lynn Marasco polished the manuscript with impressive skill and sensitivity. Many others provided essential support.

In my book's earlier stages, I benefited greatly from critiques by Margaret Todd Maitland and Lawrence Sutin. At a later phase of the process, I was heartened by affirmative prepublication reviews by Laurie Hertzel and Professors Priscilla Ferguson Clement and Sheila Coghill. My thanks to Priscilla Ferguson Clement also for the book's afterword.

Many people who trace their beginnings to the Owatonna, Minnesota, orphanage have shared their stories with me, most notably Yvonne Pearson Grondin, who also helped me remember my own story. Others provided historical material and pointed me to other sources. Chief among them was Harvey Ronglien, who, along with his wife, Maxine Ronglien, conceived and achieved a memorial to the Owatonna children. They continue to raise funds for historic preservation of the former orphanage site.

The citizens of Owatonna, Minnesota, deserve praise for the interest they have maintained in that institution through all its incarnations, and for their current support of the state school restoration project.

Most of all, loving thanks to my family. Writing a book about one's own life requires of them an extra measure of trust and understanding.

It is such a joy to say this to my husband: My deepest thanks to you, Glenn, for being there for me every step of the way. You made the work of it less work, and the fun of it more fun.

Afterword

Priscilla Ferguson Clement

Between the eighteenth century, when the first orphan asylums opened in what would become the United States, and the 1940s, when most ceased to exist, thousands of children spent portions of their lives in orphanages. Some of these children and countless others lived in foster and adoptive homes, yet comparatively few ever recorded their experiences. Donna Scott Norling is the exception. She gives us a unique child's-eye view of orphanages, foster care, and adoption. It is the purpose of this afterword to put her remarkable chronicle in historical perspective.

Government intervention in the lives of poor children has a long history. English settlers in America accepted the principles of the Elizabethan Poor Law of 1601, which permitted local governments to send orphans and children of impoverished parents unable to support their families out to learn a trade as apprentices. In North America, English colonists replicated the welfare system of their homeland when they authorized local officials, usually known as overseers of the poor, to expend tax dollars on poor children. Overseers assisted poor, widowed mothers so they could support their young children at home or paid families in the local community to care for friendless, orphaned infants. They saved tax monies and provided for the future of older impoverished children—orphaned or not—by placing them in the homes of farmers or artisans to work in exchange for room, board, medical care, and education in a trade. In the colonial era poor youths from their early to their late teens lived in families other than their own, but so too did virtually all other young people. It was then customary for families to place their own adolescent children with neighboring farmers or artisans so that boys could learn a trade and girls could learn domestic skills. Colonial Americans apparently sought to forestall youthful rebellion against parental control and keep children in submission to adults by sending their sons and daughters to live with and work for neighbors.

In the colonial period, welfare programs for poor youngsters did not single them out for family placement or an education different from that of more well off children, but all that changed in the late eighteenth century. By then prosperous American parents had adopted new ideas about child rearing made popular in Europe by John Locke and Jean-Jacques Rousseau. Locke stressed the pliability of young children and the importance of continued parental involvement in their upbringing, while Rousseau encouraged parents to tailor a child's education to his or her individual needs. Middle- and upper-class parents ceased to place their children with other families and instead kept them at home where their mothers could teach them appropriate values and develop their unique abilities. By the mid-nineteenth century, middle-class fathers could afford to support their wives and children in private homes in relative comfort. The beginnings of industrialization in the United States had opened to educated middle-class men well-paying jobs as accountants, lawyers, and business managers. To secure similar opportunities for their sons, prosperous parents kept boys at home until their late teens or early twenties so they could attend school for enough years to qualify for good jobs in business. Middle-class daughters also required an extended education to prepare them to be responsible mothers and teachers.

Industrialization improved the opportunities of middle-class parents and their children, but not those of many working-class families.

Until the First World War, most wage labor jobs in industry paid men so little that they they could not support their families on their earnings alone. Working-class wives took in boarders and did sewing in their homes, but still their families lived on the edge of poverty. Consequently, poor parents often required their children to work outside the home to help support the family. Accidents, illness, and periodic unemployment were constant threats to working-class families. Economic depressions were all too frequent in the nineteenth century and did not end there: the Great Depression of the 1930s was as prolonged and serious as the depression of the 1890s. When illness, death, or extended unemployment broke up their families, children often came to the attention of public and private welfare officials.

In the late eighteenth century and into the nineteenth, local public welfare authorities continued to place poor children with local families who required their labor, but those who were too young to work now ended up not in the homes of neighbors but in almshouses—public institutions for the poor. Almshouses first appeared in cities but subsequently spread to rural areas as well. They were catchall institutions that housed a variety of poor people, including sick, disabled, and mentally ill adults along with children. By the nineteenth century, welfare programs for poor children singled them out as different from more prosperous youngsters who rarely went to work before their late teens and seldom lived in institutions.

Almshouses were so awful and the plight of poor children so pitiful that prosperous, concerned Americans sought an alternative. By the third decade of the nineteenth century and continuing into the twentieth, groups of philanthropic citizens throughout the country founded orphan asylums to provide more comfortable homes for poor children than could their parents or the almshouses. Some small, private orphanages boarded youngsters temporarily during family emergencies. Other orphanages, including large public ones founded in the late nineteenth century at Coldwater, Michigan, and Owatonna, Minnesota, required parents to relinquish to asylum officials legal control over their children until they were eighteen to twenty-one years of age. Middle-class founders of these and many other orphanages were highly critical of poor parents for not adequately providing for their children. Few appreciated the economic problems faced by working-class Americans. Instead, they sought to "save" poor children by permanently separating them from their families, thereby allowing boys and girls to begin new and, it was hoped, more prosperous lives. To this end, most orphanages tried to place their wards with families that would feed, clothe, and educate them to adulthood, often in exchange for the youngsters' labor. Of course, such placement was economical and saved more prosperous citizens from having to support poor children in asylums indefinitely, and it had a long history. Still, in the nineteenth and twentieth centuries, only poor children like Patty and Duane Pearson were likely to end up in families other than their own.

Orphanages were one of the few forms of welfare available for needy parents before the passage of the Social Security Act in 1935. Some received a little cash, food, fuel, or medicine from local public officials, but there were few worker compensation programs before World War I, no health insurance ever, and no unemployment or old age insurance payments made until the late 1930s. In the absence of public assistance to their families, poor children often entered orphanages, where, ironically, full orphans were rare. Many of the children had one living parent, usually their mothers, and by the 1920s the majority of children in orphanages had two living parents, as did the Pearson children.

Children came to orphanages in many ways, but by the early twentieth century, juvenile courts referred most of them as was the case with the Pearson children. The first juvenile courts opened in Chicago in 1899 and in Denver in 1901. They grew in popularity and spread to most major cities in the United States. Their creators intended the courts to remove young criminals from adult courts and adjudicate their cases in a more child-friendly environment. Predicated on the belief that poverty leads to delinquency, juvenile courts cast a wide net to ferret out poor children before they committed a crime, to intervene early in their lives. Sometimes intervention involved supervision of youngsters in their natural family homes by court-appointed social workers or probation officers, and sometimes removal of youngsters to orphanages or juvenile reformatories.

Children came to the attention of the juvenile court in many ways. In the case of the Pearson family, it may have been through the police who arrested Mr. Pearson, the hospital where Duane was born, or even the suggestion of a neighbor or friend of the family. (We can only suppose, for the juvenile court records of the Pearson family have been destroyed, as is often the case with "outdated" public records.) Juvenile courts typically accepted referrals from many sources. After referral, the court usually sent a probation officer or social worker in its employ to investigate the family. Social work became a "profession" only after World War I, and most of its practitioners were female.

Even had the social worker who visited the Pearson family home not found the children alone and unwilling to tell her where their mother was, she might very well have concluded that this young mother and her three children, one an infant, were not likely to be able to get by in the absence of a male breadwinner. It was the middle of a depression, and there were few decent-paying jobs available to anyone. Even should she find work, Mrs. Pearson would have to pay for child care. Her plight was typical of mothers of children in orphan asylums, most of whom were without husbands (most often as a result of death but sometimes desertion or the incarceration of the husband in a prison or mental hospital). Orphanages were one of the few welfare resources available to them. They might claim public assistance from local officials, but the amount was minimal. Between 1911 and 1919, thirty-nine states created publicly funded mothers' pensions, but they too were underfunded, even in the 1920s. Mrs. Pearson may not have been eligible for a mothers' pension since officials used moral criteria to determine eligibility: pensions typically went to widows and their children, who were obviously not responsible for their poverty, but rarely to prisoners' wives and children, who might in some way have been accomplices to the men's crimes. Even if she had been eligible for a mothers' pension, Mrs. Pearson probably could not have supported herself and three children on one, for during the Great Depression of the 1930s, with tax revenues down, public authorities paid impoverished mothers either minuscule amounts or nothing at all.

So Patty, Yvonne, and Duane entered the State Public School for Dependent and Neglected Children together. It was common for children to arrive at orphanages in sibling groups, and it is refreshing to hear how the Pearson girls stuck together, how they supported and protected one another, as many other sisters and brothers probably did as well. For a time Patty was even able to see Duane regularly. Still, orphanages did not work to keep sibling groups together. Most divided children by age and gender, as Owatonna did, and so brothers and sisters spent most of their time apart as, eventually, the Pearson children did.

Orphanage officials, highly skeptical of poor parents' ability to care for their sons and daughters (the presence of their children in an orphanage was sufficient proof of parental failure) only reluctantly admitted mothers and fathers to visit their offspring. Permitting a parental visit just once a month, as Owatonna did, was usual. Many orphanages were located well outside the cities where the parents lived, so trips to see their children were both time-consuming and costly.

Priding themselves on making good homes for children, orphanages tried to employ responsible persons to care for them. Nonetheless, late-twentieth-century experience has taught us that it is not easy to identify potential child molesters and that they often seek employment where they have easy access to youngsters. It was probably no different in the past, and Patty's experience of molestation may have been all too common. We do not know, because few children who were in such institutions have testified to having been abused. Historians have uncovered evidence of sexual abuse in juvenile reformatories, though not between employees and children. There older boys often harassed younger ones and sometimes forced sex on them.

Orphanages may not have properly screened all their employees, but they did try to hire a competent medical staff. It did not take long for officials to discover that the children they admitted were often in ill health and, without proper attention, likely to spread contagion in the institution. Epidemics of measles, diphtheria, and other childhood diseases disabled and sometimes killed young orphans and left asylums vulnerable to public criticism. Orphanages could hardly be a humane alternative to the natural families of their wards unless they provided proper medical attention. In the late nineteenth and early twentieth centuries, with better understanding of the germ theory, orphanages like Owatonna made an aggressive effort to ensure the health of their youngsters by isolating new arrivals like Patty,

Yvonne, and Duane in special wards for several weeks to be sure that they carried no diseases and removing sick children at the first sign of infection to facilities where they could be treated well apart from other children. In all likelihood, poor children received better medical care in orphanages than they did at home.

Orphanages also prided themselves on the schooling they offered youngsters. Urban public grammar schools got started in the 1830s and 1840s and were often overcrowded even in the 1870s and 1880s. They educated children nine months a year, but rural schools were usually open only three to six months a year. In contrast, virtually all orphanages maintained schools of their own, often year around, or arranged with nearby public or parochial schools to educate their charges. In institution schools, as in all elementary education classrooms of the day, female teachers were the norm. Children in orphanages had excellent school attendance records; unlike poor children living with their families, they never missed school because they had to work or tend to an ailing parent.

The first kindergartens—usually private—appeared in American cities in the late nineteenth century. Public school systems added kindergartens slowly, but orphanages like Owatonna were quick to introduce them. Preschool education socialized needy young children, whose home lives had often been disorderly, to regular habits. Presumably, as kindergartners learned to follow the clock and perform exercises at given intervals, they gained a steadiness of purpose that would later serve them well in school and in the work world.

Orphanages also made vocational education available to their charges long before it became a common offering in public schools. Officials were anxious to teach needy boys and girls how to support themselves—an education they assumed the children's impoverished parents inevitably lacked. Both in orphanages like Owatonna and in public schools, vocational education was gendered. Boys typically learned in shop classrooms how to work with tools, and in orphanages in rural areas like Owatonna, they also performed farm chores that might prove to be useful when they were placed out or released. In contrast, girls usually acquired only domestic skills such as sewing, cooking, and cleaning, for the assumption of both public school and orphanage officials was that the occupation most suitable for working-class young women was domestic service. Nonetheless, by the 1920s some public schools had introduced bookkeeping and other secretarial courses for young women, and Owatonna provided Yvonne and other girls with practical training in nursing.

Chores that youngsters like Yvonne and Patty performed in or-phanages were also gendered. Officials assigned girls domestic duties and boys more physically demanding tasks like hauling wood. This not only taught youngsters basic skills and indoctrinated them to the work ethic, it also saved the institution the cost of hiring adults to do these tasks.

Few orphanages maintained anything but a kindergarten and a grammar school. Before the 1920s, many middle-class children at-tended high schools, but working-class children typically quit after grammar school to go to work to help support their families. In the prosperous 1920s, more working-class parents earned enough to be able to forgo their children's labor and send them to school longer. As high school education became more universal, orphanages like Owatonna enrolled their teenage wards in local public high schools. Some children's asylums sent only their brightest pupils to high school and kept the rest in the institution to work. Orphanage resi-dents did not always mingle easily with other students, although some did. Often their clothes were different from their classmates'. At Owatonna their shoes were unique; in other places it was their coats, their dresses, or even their haircuts that set them off from their peers. It would be wrong, though, to assume that their fellow stu-dents consistently took advantage of orphans. They had had to make their way first in rough neighborhoods and later within an institu-tional setting. Most were perfectly able to hold their own in public high schools.

Orphanages rarely maintained high schools within their walls not only because of the expense, but also because they did not expect to retain many youngsters into their teens. Some boys and girls did stay many years in orphanages, as did Yvonne, who was released at age eighteen, but orphanages generally preferred to place children with families to get them out of the institution as soon as possible. While brothers and sisters typically entered orphanages together, rarely did officials place them out together. The experience of the Pearson children is typical. They ended up in different families, out of touch with one another and with their parents.

From the beginning, philanthropists who founded American orphanages expected to house children only until they were old enough to be placed out in families to work. Farm families were most likely to take in poor children to help out—boys in the fields, girls in the kitchen—but urban families also sought girls to do housework.

In the late nineteenth and early twentieth centuries, as critics of orphanages proliferated, the managers grew even more determined to place out their wards promptly. In 1854, Charles Loring Brace founded the New York Children's Aid Society, which began placing poor city children directly in Midwestern farm families. Brace criticized orphanages for failing to teach children the practical skills they needed to get along in the world—skills they could best learn in families. He saw no reason for needy children to spend any time in asylums; rather, they should move directly into new family homes. Brace's program, which was rather casual and included neither thorough screening of families nor much monitoring of children after placement, came under attack late in the century. Yet he convinced many Americans that poor children, like all others, should spend their childhoods in a family and not in an institution. Orphanages should be the last, not the first, resort of needy youth. The majority of child care workers agreed with him and testified to their conviction at the 1909 White House Conference on Children called by President Theodore Roosevelt. Throughout the country foster care agencies sprang up. Like the New York Children's Aid Society, they sought to place poor children directly in families, but they evaluated potential foster parents more carefully, paid them to care for the youngsters, and supervised the girls' and boys' subsequent progress.

Orphanages also attempted to place out their young charges quickly. Thus, within months of her arrival at Owatonna, Patty moved into a foster family and later into a foster group home. The fact that Patty's first placements did not work out was not unusual. Foster families could return children for any reason, and many did. Thus youngsters often moved back and forth between Owatonna and various foster families. Even today children in foster care often transfer from one family to another. While it is preferable to institutionalization, foster care has never provided all poor children with a steady, secure home life.

Early on, child care officials recognized the limitations of foster care and began to push for legal adoption of poor children by more prosperous families. Before the 1920s few states had laws permitting adoption. In England and among whites in the United States, ''family'' had long been defined almost exclusively by blood relationship. White families might be willing to take in a poor child for his or her labor, but most perceived the child as distinct and unusual, of suspect parentage and not suited to becoming a full member of the family. This attitude softened somewhat in the twentieth century and more families sought children to adopt, but not just any children. Most families proved to be willing to adopt only infants (of either sex) and very young girls—presumably because they could most easily be molded to conform to their new families: infants would not remember any but their adoptive parents, and little girls were perceived as loving and adaptable and less rebellious than boys. For these reasons, it is not surprising that of the Pearson children, baby Duane was adopted first and seven-year-old Patty second.

Until quite recently the attitude that natural children were preferable and non–home-grown youngsters were of questionable background persisted. Both child care agency practices and adoption laws reflected these popular views. Thus agencies tried to match children to families by appearance, and laws kept records sealed in order to sever an adopted child's connection with her or his natural family permanently. Legal adoption also required that a new birth certificate with the name chosen for the child by the adopting parents be issued. While there is no evidence that Owatonna officials made a physical match between Patty and the Scotts, once they adopted her, Owatonna sought to break all ties to her natural family and denied Yvonne knowledge of her sister's whereabouts. And, of course, the Scotts renamed their new daughter Donna even before they were able formally to adopt her.

While young children were excellent candidates for adoption, older boys and girls were not. With them, earlier practices continued right through the 1930s: officials placed them in families to work. Girls were especially prized as domestic servants. Until the 1920s, domestic service was the occupation of most women who worked outside their own homes. It was always risky, since servants were especially likely to suffer physical abuse and rape. Poor girls placed in isolated rural areas, without natural family members to turn to for help, were particularly in danger. Thus, it is not surprising that Patty and Yvonne observed so many teenage girls who returned to Owatonna pregnant after being placed out to work in families.

Of course, sexual abuse of children in foster families was also possible. Owatonna officials removed Patty fairly quickly from her first home. Officials also sent social workers to visit adopting families regularly and at unexpected times in order to be sure they treated their new charges properly. Yet clearly these efforts were imperfect. If Mrs. Scott, who was a good mother, could thwart the agents from visiting when it wasn't convenient for her, so probably could less loving parents avoid visits for other reasons. Finally, state welfare officials proved so anxious to get Patty—now Donna—settled into a permanent home that they abandoned their own standard requirement for a private bedroom.

While adoption and foster care for poor children continue, the last great heyday of orphanages was the 1930s, when the Pearson children entered Owatonna. After the 1909 White House Conference on Children, the growing commitment to keeping children with their families led to mothers' pension legislation and the opportunity for more needy children to remain with their natural mothers. When the Great Depression of the 1930s undermined mothers' pensions and impoverished countless two-parent families, throngs of impoverished children once again filled orphanages.

Then in 1935 Congress passed the Social Security Act and replaced state-provided mothers' pensions with a new federal program called Aid to Dependent Children. The first ADC payments were hardly generous, and many states did not award any benefits until the 1940s. Nonetheless, the program made it financially feasible for more poor women than ever before to provide for their children at home rather than be forced by economic necessity to place them in orphanages. All across the nation orphanages either went out of business altogether or were transformed into facilities for children with physical or mental disabilities or nursing homes for the aged. Owatonna became a school for educable mentally retarded children in 1945, and in 1947 its name was changed to Owatonna State School. The school closed in 1970, after public schools began to "mainstream" them into regular classrooms.

The town of Owatonna still uses many of the state public school buildings, and the townspeople have created a memorial to the thousands of youngsters who spent portions of their childhoods in this institution. Over a century after the orphanage opened, Norling's memoir gives a voice to the many children who grew up there.

Yet neither the memorial nor our sympathy for children like the Pearsons should make us sentimental about orphanages. Certainly Norling is not. Orphanages were costly to taxpayers, and today they would be even more so. For children without families able to support them, orphanages were rarely permanent homes but rather stations on the way to work, to placement in one foster home after another, or, for the comparatively fortunate, to adoptive family homes. Orphanages "worked" only because poor parents, especially mothers, had no way to protect their children from hunger and homelessness other than to turn them over to such institutions. It is not surprising that by the 1940s, when needy mothers finally had a viable alternative source of support in Aid to Dependent Children (later called Aid to Families with Dependent Children), orphanages experienced a drop in admissions. Foster care and adoption continue, but they too have serious drawbacks, as Norling's narrative reminds us. Drug- and alcohol-addicted and abusive parents probably should not have custody of their natural children, but those who are simply not able to support them financially deserve more sympathy and respect. For them and for their children, neither orphanages nor foster care nor adoption is the answer. Preserving families requires adequate welfare payments, job-training programs for parents, and access to day care and health care. When we as a nation have met these needs, we can truly say that we are protecting children from poverty.

Suggestions for Further Reading

There are several general histories of welfare for children. Among them are LeRoy Ashby, *Saving the Waifs: Reformers and Dependent Chil-*

dren, 1890-1917 (Philadelphia: Temple University Press, 1984); Robyn Muncy, *Creating a Female Dominion in American Reform, 1890-1935* (New York: Oxford University Press, 1991); Peter C. Holloran, *Boston's Wayward Children: Social Services for Homeless Children, 1830-1930* (Rutherford, N.J.: Fairleigh Dickinson University Press, 1989); Joan Gittens, *Poor Relations: The Children of the State in Illinois, 1818-1990* (Urbana: University of Illinois Press, 1994); and Homer Folks, *The Care of Destitute, Neglected, and Delinquent Children* (New York: Johnson Reprint, 1970; reprint of 1902 ed.); Robert Bremner, "Other People's Children," *Journal of Social History* 16 (Spring 1983): 83-103.

For an overview of orphanages, see Timothy Andrew Hacsi, " 'A Plain and Solemn Duty': A History of Orphan Asylums in America" (Ph.D. dissertation, University of Pennsylvania, 1993). On particular orphan asylums, see Priscilla Ferguson Clement, "With Wise and Benevolent Purpose: Poor Children and the State Public School at Owatonna, 1885-1915," *Minnesota History* 49, no. 1 (Spring 1984): 2-13; Priscilla Ferguson Clement, "Children and Charity: Orphanages in New Orleans, 1817-1914," *Louisiana History* 27, no. 4 (Fall 1986): 337-52; Hyman Bogen, *The Luckiest Orphans: A History of the Hebrew Orphan Asylum of New York* (Urbana: University of Illinois Press, 1992); Kenneth Cmiel, *A Home of Another Kind: One Chicago Orphanage and the Tangle of Child Welfare* (Chicago: University of Chicago Press, 1995); Reena Sigman Friedman, *These Are Our Children: Jewish Orphanages in the United States, 1880-1925* (Hanover, N.H.: University Press of New England, 1994); Gary Edward Polster, *Inside Looking Out: The Cleveland Jewish Orphan Asylum, 1868-1924* (Kent, Ohio: Kent State University Press, 1990); Nurith Zmora, *Orphanages Reconsidered: Child Care Institutions in Progressive Era Baltimore* (Philadelphia: Temple University Press, 1994).

On placing poor children in families, see Bruce Bellingham, " 'Little Wanderers': A Socio-Historical Study of the Nineteenth Century Origins of Child Fostering and Adoption Reform, Based on Early Records of the New York Children's Aid Society" (Ph.D. dissertation, University of Pennsylvania, 1984); Priscilla Ferguson Clement, "Families and Foster Care: Philadelphia in the Late Nineteenth Century," *Social Service Review* 53, no. 3 (September 1979):

406-20; Marilyn Irvin Holt, *The Orphan Trains: Placing Out in America* (Lincoln: University of Nebraska Press, 1992). On adoption, see Elizabeth Bartholet, *Family Bonds: Adoption and the Politics of Parenting* (Boston: Houghton Mifflin, 1993); Betty Jean Lifton, *Journey of the Adopted Self: A Quest for Wholeness* (New York: BasicBooks, 1994); Judith S. Modell, *Kinship with Strangers: Adoption and Interpretations of Kinship in American Culture* (Berkeley: University of California Press, 1994).

For historical perspectives on welfare to poor mothers, see Joanne Goodwin, *Gender, Politics, and Welfare Reform: Mothers' Pensions in Chicago, 1900-1930* (Ann Arbor: University of Michigan Press, 1991); Linda Gordon, *Pitied but not Entitled: Single Mothers and the History of Welfare, 1890-1935* (New York: Free Press, 1994); Beverly Ann Stadum, *Poor Women and Their Families: Hard Working Charity Cases, 1900-1930* (Albany: State University of New York Press, 1992).

Donna Scott Norling is a freelance writer who enjoys being involved in writers groups, politics, and her church. She and her husband live in St. Louis Park, Minnesota; they have a son and a daughter and three granddaughters.

Priscilla Ferguson Clement is associate professor of history and women's studies at Penn State University, Delaware County Campus. Her field of specialty is social welfare history and how welfare programs have affected women and children. She is the author of several articles on nineteenth-century orphanages, juvenile reformatories, and foster care programs and of *Welfare and the Poor in the Nineteenth-Century City: Philadelphia, 1800 to 1854* (1985) and *Growing Pains: Children in the United States, 1850-1890* (forthcoming 1997).